LAST MAN — One Small Step

THE LAST MAN — One Small Step

Brian K. Vaughan
Writer

Pia Guerra
Paul Chadwick
Pencillers

José Marzán, Jr.
Inker

Pamela Rambo
Colorist

Clem Robins
Letterer

J.G. Jones
Original series covers

Y: THE LAST MAN created by Brian K. Vaughan and Pia Guerra

Y: THE LAST MAN — ONE SMALL STEP
Published by DC Comics. Cover, introduction and compilation
copyright © 2004 DC Comics. All Rights Reserved.

Originally published in single magazine form as Y: THE LAST MAN 11-17.
Copyright © 2003, 2004 Brian K. Vaughan and Pia Guerra. All Rights Reserved.
All characters, their distinctive likenesses and related elements featured in
this publication are trademarks of Brian K. Vaughan and Pia Guerra. VERTIGO
is a trademark of DC Comics. The stories, characters and incidents featured in
this publication are entirely fictional. DC Comics does not read or accept
unsolicited submissions of ideas, stories or artwork.

DC Comics, 1700 Broadway, New York, NY 10019
A Warner Bros. Entertainment Company.
Printed in Canada. First Printing.
ISBN: 1-4012-0201-2
Cover illustration by J.G. Jones.

ONE MAN'S STORY...

The plague struck without warning and without mercy, all across the globe. Every mammal on Earth that bore a Y chromosome died in a matter of seconds. Out of billions of animals, only two were spared — a human named Yorick Brown, and his pet monkey, Ampersand. Why they survived is a mystery.

In the aftermath of this apocalypse, Yorick and Ampersand set out from Brooklyn to contact Yorick's mother, a U.S. congresswoman. After making their way down a devastated eastern seaboard, they found her in Washington, D.C., struggling to keep the remains of the U.S. government intact. The appearance of the last man (and monkey) provided a newly installed President with fresh hope for the future of the human race, and Yorick soon found himself on a mission to track down the cloning expert Dr. Allison Mann to help her try to prevent the species' extinction.

After briefly crossing paths with a group of man-hating radicals called the Daughters of the Amazon, Yorick and Ampersand made it to Dr. Mann's lab in Boston — accompanied by Agent 355, a member of a shadowy government security force known as the Culper Ring. There they found the bioengineer in a state of anguish, convinced that her cloning experiments had caused the plague. But while Yorick had been looking for Dr. Mann, another group was looking for *him* — a team of Israeli commandos, the most accomplished female soldiers in the world, far from home and pursuing their own agenda. After missing the Last Man in the lab, they decided to burn it to the ground.

With few other options available to them, Yorick, Ampersand, 355 and Dr. Mann set out for California to retrieve the backups of Dr. Mann's data. After bribing their way into a boxcar heading west, however, the group was set upon by thieves and forced to abandon the train outside Marrisville, Ohio — a town settled by the population of a women's prison.

Marrisville proved to be an oasis of stability in a countryside filled with anarchy, but that calm was shattered with the arrival of the Daughters of the Amazons, who had tracked down Yorick with the help of their newest member — his sister, Hero. Threatening to destroy the town unless the Last Man was turned over for execution, the Amazons' leader was instead cut down herself by the woman who had found Yorick unconscious next to the railroad tracks — an act of bravery that she paid for with her life, courtesy of Hero's archery skills. Reeling from what his sister had become, Yorick left her with the remaining Amazons in Marrisville's reopened prison, and continued west with his companions.

Now, as their train rolls slowly across the plains, a hijacked Black Hawk helicopter follows from the east, quickly closing the distance between the Last Man and a grimly determined team of Israelis. And two hundred and twenty miles above them all, three desperate humans prepare for their return voyage from space — a one-way trip that, if successful, could triple the number of men on Earth.

Marquand, Missouri
Now

WHAT KIND OF SOMETHING?

HALF A PACK.

WHEN THE HELL DID YOU START SMOKING, 355?

WHEN A PLAGUE OF BIBLICAL PROPORTIONS KILLED EVERY MAN EXCEPT FOR *YOUR* HAIRY ASS?

FAIR ENOUGH.

CAN I BUM ONE OFF YOU?

SORRY, 'RICK. THE PRESIDENT ORDERED ME TO *PROTECT* YOU, NOT TO SULLY YOUR PINK LUNGS.

SUIT YOURSELF.

HOPE THE CULPER RING TAUGHT YOU HOW TO RUB TWO STICKS TOGETHER.

IF YOU EVER TELL YOUR MOTHER ABOUT THIS, I'LL KILL YOU MYSELF.

GOD YOU'RE EASY...

"FUCK COMMUNISM"?

WHAT ARE YOU, A COSSACK?

OH, THE ENGRAVING?

IT'S FROM THIS THING I READ BACK IN HIGH SCHOOL, A, UH...A "GRAPHIC NOVEL." YOU KNOW, LIKE A COMIC BOOK?

THEY CAN SAY "FUCK" IN COMIC BOOKS?

I GUESS.

JEEZ, THEY NEVER SAID STUFF LIKE THAT IN SUPERMAN.

SUPERMAN'S JUST MAKE-BELIEVE, 355.

IN THE REAL WORLD...

...I'M THE STRONGEST MAN ON EARTH.

One Small Step

Chapter One

BRIAN K. VAUGHAN PIA GUERRA
Writer/Co-Creators/Penciller

JOSE MARZAN, JR., Inker

Clem Robins, Letterer   Pamela Rambo, Colorist
Zylonol, Separator J.G. Jones, Cover Artist
Steve Bunche, Editor

Y: THE LAST MAN CREATED BY BRIAN K. VAUGHAN AND PIA GUERRA

RELAX, DOC, IT'S JUST--

WHATEVER, BREAK'S OVER. THEY'VE APPARENTLY FINISHED REPAIRING THE LITTLE ENGINE THAT COULDN'T.

AND GET THIS ANIMAL AWAY FROM ME. IT DEFECATED IN MY *MEDICAL BAG.*

COME ON, AMPERSAND... BEFORE MRS. HYDE'S TRANSFORMATION IS COMPLETE.

GO EASY ON HIM, DR. MANN. HE'S STILL NOT OVER WHAT HAPPENED BACK IN MARRISVILLE.

355, IS THERE SOMETHING GOING *ON* BETWEEN YOU TWO?

WHO, ME AND...?

EW, NO!

THIS ISN'T *POST-COITAL,* IF THAT'S WHAT YOU'RE SUGGESTING.

WELL, IT'S JUST... BACK IN OHIO, YOU *SAID* SOMETHING. WHEN YOU WERE UNCONSCIOUS. YOU SAID...

FORGET IT.

PROBABLY JUST THE ANESTHESIA TALKING.

TRUST ME, DOCTOR, MY ONLY INTEREST IN YORICK IS KEEPING HIM OUT OF *TROUBLE*...

HEY, YOU!

ME?

YEAH... WHAT'S THAT BEARD MADE OUT OF?

OH.

IT'S SPIRIT GUM AND, UH... HORSEHAIR.

THOUGHT SO. YOU SHOULD REALLY TRY USING YOUR *OWN* HAIR. SAVE SOME CLIPPINGS NEXT TIME YOU GET IT CUT. LOOKS MORE NATURAL.

YEAH.

THAT'S WHAT PEOPLE KEEP TELLING ME.

SO, YOU GOT A GIRL-FRIEND?

OR ARE YOU A WORKING GIRL LIKE ME?

GIRLFRIEND.

WE'RE ENGAGED, ACTUALLY... MORE OR LESS.

GOOD, I WAS AFRAID YOU WERE GONNA TAKE ALL OF MY CUSTOMERS ON THIS LINE.

SERIOUSLY, YOUR LADY'S LUCKY TO HAVE SOMEONE AS DEDICATED AS YOU. BIND THOSE BREASTS A LITTLE TIGHTER AND YOU'LL ALMOST BE PASSABLE.

...THANKS?

ANYWAY, HAVE A SAFE TRIP.

KEEP AN EYE OUT FOR AMAZONS!

WILL DO.

YOU AND ME, LITTLE BUDDY...ADRIFT IN AN OCEAN OF ESTROGEN.

ER AH HA

14

ROCKS AND TREES, ROCKS AND TREES...

I CAN'T WAIT TO GET OUT OF THIS GODDAMN CABOOSE FOR GOOD.

DON'T GET TOO EXCITED, YORICK. EVEN WHEN WE *DO* REACH SAN FRANCISCO, IT'S NOT LIKE WE'LL HAVE TIME FOR CRACKED CRAB AND JET SKIS.

I HAVE HUNDREDS OF TESTS TO PERFORM ON YOU...PRESUMING MY LATE DAUGHTER'S EMBRYONIC CELLS ARE STILL INTACT FOR COMPARISON.

DAUGHTER? I THOUGHT THE CLONE YOU GAVE BIRTH TO WAS A *MALE*.

WHAT? OF COURSE, THAT'S WHAT I--

THUNK

THE HELL...?

SOUNDS LIKE SOMETHING HIT OUR ROOF.

I'LL CHECK IT OUT.

I'M COMING WITH YOU.

NO!

IF HE TRIES TO FOLLOW ME, DO WHAT WE DISCUSSED.

I'M ON IT.

WHAT THE FUCK?

OH, YOU GUYS STINK.

OOF!

FUCK!

JESUS CHRIST, HERE WE GO...

...AGAIN?

USE MY HELP, PLEASE!

I SAVE LIFE AND YOU LET ME INSIDE YOUR TRAIN, DA?

THAT MEDAL... HOW THE HELL DID YOU GET A GOLD STAR?

I WAS GOOD LITTLE GIRL IN SCHOOL.

BUT THAT'S RESERVED FOR HEROES OF THE RUSSIAN FEDERA--

NO MORE KICKING, NO MORE QUESTIONS. WE ARE FRIENDS AND EVEN, OKAY?

355!

UM... EVERYTHING COOL UP HERE?

GODDAMMIT, YORICK.

HOW...?

HEY, I RECOGNIZE HER.

SHE'S THAT STOWAWAY THEY THREW OFF THE TRAIN BACK IN MARRISVILLE.

WHO... WHO IS THIS MAN?

HE'S NOT THE PERSON YOU'RE AFTER?

NO, I AM GOING TO KANSAS FOR...FOR...

IT IS VERY HARD TO BE EXPLAINING FOR ME IN YOUR LANGUAGE.

‹THEN TRY IT IN YOUR TONGUE.›

‹YOU SPEAK RUSSIAN?›

‹NOT FOR LONG TIME.›

‹MY GRAMMAR IS A LITTLE, um... FROGGY?›

〈THANK CHRIST! I SOUND LIKE A FUCKING *RETARD* WHEN I TRY TO SPEAK ENGLISH.〉

〈SLOW DOWN. WHO *IS* YOU?〉

〈MY NAME'S NATALYA ZAMYATIN.〉

〈I WAS SENT BY WHAT'S LEFT OF THE GOVERNMENT TO RETRIEVE OUR COUNTRY'S ONLY LIVING MALE, A COSMONAUT ON BOARD THE INTERNATIONAL SPACE STATION.〉

〈WHAT?〉

HEY, COMRADES, CAN SOMEONE TRANSLATE THIS OR--

〈FOR MONTHS, HE'S BEEN TRAPPED INSIDE THE I.S.S. WITH TWO OF YOUR ASTRO-NAUTS, ONE MALE AND ONE FEMALE.〉

〈HOW CAN YOU BE SURE HE'S STILL ALIVE?〉

〈WELL, WE LOST HAM CONTACT A FEW WEEKS AGO, BUT MY PEOPLE HAVE TALKED TO BOTH MEN SINCE JULY, SO WE KNOW THEY SURVIVED THE PLAGUE.〉

〈THEY'VE BEEN WAITING FOR *NASA* TO SEND A SHUTTLE TO RESCUE THEM...BUT HOUSTON APPARENTLY DOESN'T HAVE THE RESOURCES TO MAKE THAT HAPPEN.〉

〈THEN HOW ARE *YOU* PLANNING TO GET UP THERE?〉

〈I'M NOT.〉

〈THEY'RE COMING DOWN HERE.〉

YOU'VE HEARD THE HORROR STORIES, RIGHT? THE SOYUZ ISN'T A LIFE-BOAT, IT'S A DEATHTRAP.

WELL, WE'RE OBVIOUSLY NOT BEING SENT THAT LIMO WE REQUESTED, AND I'D RATHER BITE IT IN SOME CORNFIELD THAN SUFFOCATE INSIDE THIS JUNKHEAP.

EVEN IF WE *DON'T* CRASH, HOW CAN WE BE SURE THAT WHATEVER KILLED ALL THE MEN DOWN THERE WON'T KILL *YOU* THE SECOND WE LAND?

WE CAN'T, BUT WE'RE TAKING EVERY PRECAUTION POSSIBLE, CIBA.

WE'RE GOING DOWN IN SUITS, AND VLAD'S CONTACT IS SUPPOSED TO BE WAITING AT OUR E.L.Z. TO ESCORT US TO THE HOT SUITE AS SOON AS WE BLOW THE LATCH.

TRUE, COMMANDER...

...BUT FIRST WE MUST SURVIVE REENTRY.

SPEED LIMIT 1750

28 MILL

VLAD. SORRY, I THOUGHT YOU WERE STILL IN THE HEAD, TRIMMING THAT NEW SOUP STRAINER OF YOURS.

LISTEN, WHAT I WAS SAYING... IT HAS NOTHING TO DO WITH MY FAITH IN YOU AS A PILOT.

NOR SHOULD IT BE MY ABILITIES WHICH CONCERN YOU.

BECAUSE OF CHEMICAL DEGRADATION IN HYDRAZINE FUEL, SOYUZ WAS DESIGNED TO BE STORED IN SPACE FOR MAXIMUM OF SIX MONTHS..

OUR VESSEL HAS NOT BEEN REPLACED IN MORE THAN NINE.

SURE, BUT WE'VE GOT SOME WIGGLE ROOM WITH THOSE NUMBERS, RIGHT?

RUSSIAN ENGINEERS ARE NOT BIG ON "WIGGLE ROOM," SIR.

SO HOW CAN WE TELL IF THE PROPELLANT'S CORRODED ANY OF OUR SOYUZ'S DEEP PLUMBING?

ONLY ONE WAY TO KNOW FOR CERTAIN...

...IF OUR CABIN BURSTS INTO FLAMES WHEN WE ENTER ATMOSPHERE.

THIS JUST KEEPS GETTING BETTER AND BETTER...

25

Marquand, Missouri
Two Hours Later

DID YOU KNOW SHAKESPEARE COINED THAT PHRASE?

WHAT?

"WILD-GOOSE CHASE," I MEAN.

ORIGINALLY, IT DESCRIBED AN UNPREDICTABLE PATH TAKEN BY ONE INDIVIDUAL AND FOLLOWED BY ANOTHER...ENDING WHEN THE FIRST IS INEVITABLY CAUGHT.

MY SPOUSE LOVED TO POINT OUT THAT ITS MODERN USAGE IS REALLY A PESSIMISTIC MISINTERPRETATION OF--

ENOUGH! FOR MONTHS, YOU HAVE BORED ME WITH THIS PEDANTIC NONSENSE, WHILE GIVING ME NO USEFUL INFORMATION. I HAVE YET TO EVEN LEARN YOUR REAL NAME!

ALTER, BE PATIENT. I'VE TOLD YOU EVERYTHING YOU NEED TO KNOW TO FIND THE LAST MAN ON EARTH, AND YOU'RE CLOSE.

I'M NOT SURE HOW SECURE THIS FREQUENCY IS, SO I CAN'T SAY MORE THAN--

THAT EXCUSE IS NO LONGER ACCEPTABLE. GIVE ME A REASON TO CONTINUE TRUSTING YOU, OR I AM TAKING MY TROOPS BACK TO TEL AVIV.

NOW, FOR THE LAST TIME, WHO ARE YOU?

GOOD LORD, ISN'T IT OBVIOUS, ALTER?

THE LAST MAN ON EARTH IS YOUR *CHILD*?

UNLESS I *IMAGINED* THOSE TWENTY-SIX HOURS I WAS IN LABOR.

MY NAME IS REPRESENTATIVE JENNIFER BROWN. I'M--

REPRESENTATIVE? YOU'RE A U.S. *CONGRESSWOMAN*? THEN, WHY THE HELL DID YOU ASK *ISRAEL* FOR HELP? YOUR OWN MILITARY IS--

--STILL IN DISARRAY, ALTER, AS YOU'VE SEEN. I KNEW *YOU* WERE THE ONLY WOMAN WITH THE SKILLS AND RESOURCES TO RETRIEVE MY SON.

YOUR PREDECESSOR WAS...HE WAS A DEAR FRIEND OF MINE. LIEUTENANT-GENERAL YEHUDA ALWAYS SPOKE VERY HIGHLY OF YOU.

BESIDES, I'VE RUN OUT OF *AMERICANS* I CAN TRUST.

EXPLAIN.

I ASSURE YOU, THE NETWORK MY PEOPLE CREATED IS SECURE. OUR FREQUENCY IS--

YES, YES, FINE. IT HAPPENED SHORTLY AFTER MY SON LEFT WASHINGTON...

I LEARNED THE ORGANIZATION THAT HAD SWORN TO *PROTECT* YORICK WASN'T MADE UP OF ALTRUISTIC SERVANTS OF THE EXECUTIVE BRANCH, AS OUR NEW PRESIDENT HAD LED ME TO BELIEVE.

THIS "CULPER RING" IS ACTUALLY A GROUP OF THUGS AND... AND *ASSASSINS*, A GLORIFIED DIRTY TRICKS CREW. FOR DECADES, THEY'VE COMMITTED ATROCITIES FOR CORRUPT ADMINISTRATIONS.

AND YOU NOW SUSPECT THAT THIS GROUP HAS, WHAT, *KIDNAPPED* YOUR SON?

ONE OF THEIR AGENTS, YES... "355". I'M NOT SURE WHAT HER AGENDA IS, BUT I KNOW THAT SHE RECENTLY TRANSPORTED YORICK TO YOUR CURRENT LOCATION.

YOU ORIGINALLY SAID THEY WERE LOOKING FOR SOME GENETICIST IN *BOSTON*. WHAT MAKES YOU THINK YOUR SON AND HIS CAPTOR ARE NOW HERE IN *MISSOURI*?

THERE'S A CHANCE THEY MAY HAVE JUST BEEN PASSING THROUGH, ALTER. SEE, AN ASSOCIATE IN THE SECRET SERVICE ENCOURAGED ME TO PLANT A *TRACKING DEVICE* ON YORICK BEFORE HE LEFT.

WITH THE SATELLITES DOWN, SHE'S BEEN TRIANGULATING USING WHATEVER RADIO TOWERS ARE AVAILABLE, AND IT SOMETIMES TAKES A FEW *HOURS* TO GET A LOCK.

EITHER WAY, HOW CAN YOU BE CERTAIN THIS BEACON HASN'T BEEN FOUND AND REMOVED?

BECAUSE WE HID IT INSIDE YORICK'S MONKEY.

HIS *WHAT*?

GRR AK AK

One Small Step
Chapter Two

BRIAN K. VAUGHAN   PIA GUERRA
Writer/Co-Creators/Penciller

JOSE MARZAN, JR., Inker

Clem Robins, Letterer   Pamela Rambo, Colorist
Zylonol, Separator J.G. Jones, Cover Artist
Steve Bunche, Editor

Y: THE LAST MAN CREATED BY BRIAN K. VAUGHAN AND PIA GUERRA

Oldenbrook, Kansas
Ten Hours Later

IF WHAT NATALYA SAYS IS TRUE, A SOYUZ ESCAPE VESSEL IS ABOUT TO LAND WITH ONE FEMALE AND TWO MALES INSIDE. TWO *LIVING* MALES.

THOSE ASTRONAUTS ARE GOING TO NEED MY PROTECTION AND YOUR MEDICAL ATTENTION.

AND MY DISARMING WIT!

SERIOUSLY, DOC, LET YOUR UNFEELING CYBORG BRAIN RELEASE A LITTLE SEROTONIN FOR ONCE. THIS IS A MIRACLE!

NO, THIS IS A *SHAM.*

ANYONE WHO'S WATCHED AN HOUR'S WORTH OF DISCOVERY CHANNEL KNOWS THAT THE SOYUZ ALWAYS LANDS IN THE *KAZAKH STEPPES* OUT-SIDE OF RUSSIA...

...NOT IN THE MIDDLE OF SOME ALFALFA FIELD IN BUMFUCK, KANSAS.

NO, KAZAKHSTAN IS *NO POSSIBLE!*

AKTAU MAKE *POISON!* AKTAU BRING DEATH!

WAIT, REWIND. WHAT'S *AKTAU?*

IT'S A NUCLEAR POWER PLANT.

NO. NOT ANOTHER *CHERNOBYL.*

WORSE. MY GOVERNMENT THINK POSSIBLE *ONE MILLION* WOMAN DEAD. NUMBERS WILL BECOME MORE WHEN CANCER BLOWS TO RUSSIA.

OF COURSE, IF I'M NO ABLE TO BRING BACK OUR COSMONAUT IN SAFETY, MY COUNTRY HAS MORE TO WORRY ABOUT FOR FUTURE THAN *DISEASE.*

⟨NATALYA, I THOUGHT KAZAKHSTAN TOOK THEIR REACTOR, UM, WHAT'S THE RUSSIAN WORD FOR...?⟩

⟨"OFFLINE"? YEAH, SO DID WE. BUT BEFORE THE PLAGUE, MALE OFFICIALS WERE APPARENTLY OPER-ATING IT IN SECRET FOR PROFIT.⟩

⟨WHILE RUSSIA WAS WORKING ITS ASS OFF TO SHUT DOWN ALL OF OUR PLANTS, KAZAKHSTAN'S CORE WAS *MELT-ING DOWN.* ONE LAST "FUCK YOU" FROM A CORRUPT BUREAUCRACY.⟩

JESUS, WHAT A NIGHTMARE. ALL THOSE PEOPLE LIVED THROUGH THE PLAGUE...ONLY TO DIE IN SOME STUPID ACCIDENT?

IS HORRIBLE TRAGEDY, YES, BUT AT LEAST WOMEN HAD EACH OTHER, YORICK.

MY COUNTRY HAS SAYING, "EVEN DEATH IS BEAUTIFUL, IF YOU ARE NOT ALONE."

YOU SAY SO.

355, IF THAT HAPPENS TO ONE OF *OUR* REACTORS...

IT WON'T. MY COLLEAGUES HAVE BEEN DECOMMISSIONING PLANTS FOR MONTHS NOW, ALL ACROSS THE COUNTRY.

TRUST ME, THE CULPER RING IS TAKING CARE OF *EVERY-THING.*

International Space Station
Now

COMMANDER, YOU...YOU MUST FORGIVE ME.

I HAVE NO IDEA WHAT OVER-CAME ME.

YEAH, I'M I'M SORRY TOO, VLAD.

IT MUST BE THE OXYGEN DEPRIVATION, CIBA.

IT'S MAKING US *PSYCHOTIC*.

WELL, LET'S TRY TO KEEP IT TOGETHER, GENTLE-MEN. I KNOW IT FEELS LIKE WE'VE BEEN STUCK IN THIS THING TOGETHER FOREVER...

3,298 TRIPS AROUND THAT GOD-DAMN BLUE BALL.

TWICE AS MANY SHITTY POKER GAMES.

...BUT IN A FEW HOURS, IT'LL ALL BE OVER.

ONE WAY OR ANOTHER.

OKAY, BUT EVEN IF THESE THEORETICAL SPACEMEN REALLY *DID* ESCAPE THE PLAGUE, HOW DO WE KNOW IT WON'T AFFECT THEM ONCE THEY TOUCH DOWN?

WE DON'T. THIS IS WHY MY BOSSES ORDER SOYUZ TO LAND BY YOUR COUNTRY'S NEW, HOW DO YOU SAY...

IS IT "WARM ROOM"?

OUR *HOT SUITE?* THE RUSSIANS *KNEW* ABOUT IT?

K.G.B. IS DEAD, FRIEND, BUT OUR INTELLIGENCE IS NOT.

UM, I REALIZE MY USELESS B.A. IS SHOWING ...BUT WHAT THE HELL IS A HOT SUITE?

IT'S A GROUP OF LEVEL FOUR BIO-SAFETY ROOMS, SUPPOSEDLY IMPERVIOUS TO ANY INFECTIOUS AGENTS FROM THE OUTSIDE WORLD AND BLAH, BLAH, BLAH.

I KNEW THERE WAS ONE AT FORT DETRICK, BUT WE'RE IN THE MIDDLE OF *NOWHERE.*

THE GOVERNMENT HID A MASSIVE FACILITY OUT HERE FOR HIGH-RANKING OFFICIALS TO RETREAT TO IN CASE OF BIOLOGICAL ATTACKS TO MAJOR CITIES.

THEY *DID?* DO WE KNOW IF ANY DUDES WERE INSIDE THIS THING *BEFORE* THE PLAGUE HIT?

NOPE... BUT I GUESS WE'RE ABOUT TO FIND OUT.

VRRNNN

‹FORGET ABOUT REFUELING, PILOT.›

‹WE'RE NOT FAR FROM THE NEW COORDINATES THE AMERICAN PROVIDED.›

‹MY, MISSOURI YESTERDAY AND KANSAS TODAY? LET US PRAY WE HAVE NOT ONCE AGAIN "NARROWLY MISSED" THE LAST BOY ON EARTH.›

‹SADIE, A MOMENT OF YOUR TIME, PLEASE.›

‹IF YOU EVER AGAIN TAKE THAT TONE WITH ME IN FRONT OF MY SOLDIERS...›

‹...I WILL HAVE TO ASK YOU TO STEP OUTSIDE.›

‹I APOLOGIZE, LIEUTENANT-GENERAL, BUT I'M BEGINNING TO SUSPECT THAT YOU DRAGGED US ON THIS SCAVENGER HUNT SIMPLY BECAUSE YOU'D GROWN *BORED* WITH PEACE IN ISRAEL.›

‹YOU'RE WRONG.›

‹I'M DOING WHAT'S BEST FOR OUR PEOPLE.›

‹WORKING AS AN ERRAND GIRL FOR SOME AMERICAN POLITICIAN?›

‹NO, SEEING THAT THE ONLY FUNCTIONING *SPERM FACTORY* DOESN'T FALL INTO THE HANDS OF THE ENEMY.›

‹YOU KEEP USING THAT TERM, "THE ENEMY."›

‹BUT YOU TAUGHT ME THAT EUPHEMISMS ARE ONLY FOR THOSE WHO FEEL *GUILT* ABOUT WHAT THEY'RE DESCRIBING. IF YOUR CONSCIENCE IS CLEAR, ALTER, SAY WHAT YOU MEAN...›

‹ARABS.›

〈THAT'S NOT WHAT THIS IS ABOUT. MY ONLY CONCERN IS *TERROR*. HAMAS, ISLAMIC JIHAD...〉

〈THOSE GROUPS DON'T NEED *MEN* TO BLOW UP BUSES, ALTER I A...A *FEMALE* SUICIDE BOMBER KILLED MY BROTHER-IN-LAW!〉

〈THEN YOU UNDER-STAND THE NEED FOR VIGILANCE.〉

〈NO, I DON'T! THERE HASN'T BEEN A SINGLE BOMBING SINCE THE MEN DIED!〉

〈AND I INTEND TO KEEP IT THAT WAY.〉

〈HOW, BY REUNITING SOME RANDOM YOUNG MAN WITH HIS *MOTHER*?〉

〈DON'T BE AN IDIOT, SADIE. I HAVE NO INTENTION OF RETURNING YORICK TO THAT GULLIBLE SIMPLETON.〉

〈THE WAY SHE LOOKS AFTER HER SON, THAT WOULD BE TANTAMOUNT TO HANDING HIM DIRECTLY TO *HEZBOLLAH*.〉

〈THEN...WHAT *ARE* YOU PLANNING TO DO WITH THE BOY?〉

〈SET US DOWN HERE, PILOT.〉

〈WE'LL GO IN THE REST OF THE WAY ON FOOT.〉

〈IT'S IMPORTANT TO MAINTAIN THE ELEMENT OF SURPRISE.〉

SO. YOU, ehh... CHILD OF POLITICS?

WELL, MY MOM'S IN WASHINGTON, IF THAT'S WHAT YOU MEAN.

THIS IS HOW YOU STILL LIVE? SHE GIVES YOU SOME KIND OF ANECDOTE?

AN *ANTIDOTE?* NO, WHY WOULD SHE HAVE A...

WAIT, YOU DON'T THINK THE AMERICAN *GOVERNMENT* CAUSED THE PLAGUE, DO YOU?

MY SISTERS IN MILITARY SUSPECT POSSIBLY. I'M NO SURE *WHAT* TO THINK, YORICK.

SWELL, WE LOSE ALL THE MEN, BUT AT LEAST WE GET THE GODDAMN *COLD WAR* BACK.

ANYWAY, I'M STILL GLAD WE FOUND YOU, NATALYA.

YOU BROUGHT THE FIRST POTEN- TIALLY GOOD NEWS I'VE HEARD SINCE MY LIFE TURNED INTO A BAD *OUTER LIMITS* EPISODE.

COME, SMALL PART OF YOU IS SADDENED YOU MIGHT NOT BE AS... AS *SPECIAL* NOW, DA?

45

UM, WHY ARE YOU UNBUTTON-ING...?

YOUR COUNTRY SO BEAUTIFUL, BUT TOO FUCK-ING HOT.

ALWAYS THE HEAT...

NATALYA, I DON'T MEAN TO BE RUDE, BUT COULD YOU, UH, STAY AS CLOTHED AS POSSIBLE AROUND ME?

〈LORD, I NEVER THOUGHT I WOULD MISS MOSCOW.〉

〈THE WAY THE MEN'S BODIES LITTERED RED SQUARE ...THEY LOOKED LIKE CHILDREN, MAKING ANGELS IN THE SNOW.〉

〈AND I REMEMBER FINDING YOU, SWEET RODYA. THE IMAGE OF YOUR FACE, FROZEN IN MY MIND...〉

ALSO, WOULD YOU MIND NOT MUTTERING TO YOURSELF IN RUSSIAN? YOUR ACCENT IS DISTURB-INGLY SEXY.

IT'S JUST, I'VE GOT THIS GIRL I'M TRY-ING REALLY HARD TO STAY LOYAL TO, BUT THE FLESH IS WEAK, AS THEY SAY, AND I'M ONLY--

SCREECH

UNF!

FWAP

YOU SURE ABOUT THAT, OLD MacDONALD?

IT'S A *SECRET* INSTALLATION, YORICK.

IT'S NOT SUPPOSED TO LOOK LIKE THE PENTAGON.

YEAH, BUT A *BARN?*

THAT'S WHERE BANDITS *GO* TO HIDE BEFORE THEY INEVITABLY GET *SHOT* TO DEATH.

JOHN WILKES BOOTH WAS KILLED INSIDE A BARN.

SERIOUSLY, HAVEN'T WE BEEN THROUGH ENOUGH SIEGES ALREADY?

WELL, SEEING AS WE'RE NEITHER OLD-TIMEY OUT-LAWS OR REBEL ASSASSINS, I THINK WE'RE IN THE CLEAR.

AND SINCE WHEN DID *YOU* START ENCOURAGING MAGIC LAD?

SORRY, THREE-FIFTY, BUT I'M STILL FINDING ALL OF THIS A LITTLE HARD TO SWALLOW.

NO, IS TRUE! IS EXACTLY AS F.S.B. DESCRIBE TO ME!

FINE, BUT IF THERE ARE ANY *PIGS* IN THERE--

MALE!

WHOA! EASY, THELMA AND LOUISE!

IT'S JUST DECONTAMINATE.

WE HAVE TO GET THIS MAN TO A STAGING AREA!

NO YOU DON'T. THE KID'S TOTALLY IMMUNE. WE'RE NOT HERE ABOUT HIM.

WHAT THE HELL DO YOU MEAN?

SHE MEANS DON'T PUT AWAY THE E.T. GEAR YET, LADIES.

≶SPTOO≶

YOU'RE ABOUT TO GET SOME OUT-OF-TOWN VISITORS.

YORICK BROWN...

50

...AND THROUGH THE PRAYERS OF ST. NICHOLAS THE WONDERWORKER, AND OF ST. NIKITA OF NOVGOROD, DELIVER US SAFELY TO OUR SISTERS BELOW. IN THE NAME OF THE FATHER...

...AND OF THE SON...

...AND OF THE HOLY GHOST.

OR DO WE SAY HOLY *SPIRIT?* I...I HAVEN'T DONE THIS SINCE I WAS *EIGHT.*

I *LOVE* YOU, CIBA. YOU, *TOO,* VLAD.

I'M UNDOCKING NOW, COMMANDER. WE'RE FREE.

Oldenbrook, Kansas
Now

DID... DID YOU *MAKE* THEM?

THEY'RE NOT CLONES, IDIOT.

THEY'RE *TWINS*.

DOCTOR, MY NAME'S HEATHER HARTLE. THIS IS MY SISTER, HEIDI. WE'RE GENETICISTS.

YOUR *JAMA* PIECE ON ORGAN BLUEPRINTING MADE ME CRY.

I'M GUESSING YOU'RE NOT SQUATTERS HERE.

NO, WE'RE EMPLOYEES OF THE HOT SUITE.

THE *ONLY* EMPLOYEES. THE REST OF THE STAFF TOOK OFF MONTHS AGO.

YOU MEAN, THERE AREN'T ANY *MEN* ALIVE IN THERE?

NONE OF THE POLITICIANS WHO HAD THIS AS THEIR DESIGNATED *C.O.G.* SITE EVER SHOWED UP. AND ONLY WOMEN EVER WORKED HERE.

MALES HAVE... *TROUBLE* WITH THE ISOLATION.

FUCKING...

FUCK.

I AM SORRY, YORICK, BUT YOUR HOPE IS NOT BEING GONE YET.

IS WHAT HE SAID *TRUE?*

THERE ARE STILL PEOPLE ALIVE ON THE SPACE SHUTTLE?

YOUR GUESS IS AS GOOD AS MINE. I'M JUST GOING ALONG FOR THE RIDE.

LISTEN, WE NEED TO SECURE THIS FACILITY BEFORE THE *SOYUZ* TOUCHES DOWN. IF YOU REFUSE TO LET US INSIDE, MY EXECUTIVE S.C.I. CLEARANCE AUTHORIZES ME TO--

RELAX, LADY. HOUSING PEOPLE IS OUR RAISON D'ETRE. WE'VE BEEN WAITING A *YEAR* FOR SOMETHING LIKE THIS.

YEAH, MI CASA, ETC.

I'D LOVE TO RUN A FEW TESTS ON THE BOY.

JESUS, KILL ME NOW...

TSE'ELON, LO!

⟨WHAT THE HELL ARE YOU DOING? DO YOU WANT TO COMPROMISE OUR POSITION?⟩

⟨I *WANT* TO STOP YOU FROM OFFING THE LAST FUCKING MAN ON EARTH!⟩

⟨CALM DOWN, SADIE, YOU KNOW THE SCOPES ARE MORE POWERFUL THAN OUR SHIT BINOCULARS. OR HAVE YOU FORGOTTEN *EVERYTHING* I TAUGHT YOU ABOUT RECONNAISSANCE?⟩

⟨RECONNAISSANCE? SO YOU *WEREN'T* GOING TO SHOOT HIM?⟩

⟨DO YOU THINK I'M *COMPLETELY* MAD?⟩

⟨THEN...WHAT *ARE* WE GOING TO DO WITH THE KID, ALTER?⟩

⟨WE'RE TAKING HIM TO *ISRAEL*.⟩

‹IF WE CAN FIND A WAY TO DO SOMETHING ABOUT HIS CAPTORS.›

‹THIS "CULPER RING" GIRL YORICK'S MOTHER WARNED US ABOUT SEEMS TO HAVE PICKED UP SOME KIND OF MERCENARY, LOOKS LIKE EX-SPETSNAZ.›

‹WAIT, WE'RE GOING TO KIDNAP YORICK FROM HIS KIDNAPPERS?›

‹YOU'RE THE ONE WHO'S SO CONCERNED ABOUT THE "FUTURE OF ISRAEL," NO?›

‹OF COURSE, BUT HOW ARE YOU GOING TO CONVINCE SOME AMERICAN GOY TO REPOPULATE OUR HOMELAND?›

‹PERHAPS WE'LL LOCK HIM IN A ROOM WITH SEVENTY-TWO VIRGINS. I'VE HEARD THAT'S SOME MEN'S IDEA OF HEAVEN.›

‹WHY ARE YOU TALKING ABOUT HIM LIKE HE'S A TERRORIST? HE'S AN INNOCENT BOY!›

‹NONE OF US IS INNOCENT.›

‹OH, SAVE THAT NONSENSE FOR THE NEW GIRLS.›

‹WHAT ARE YOU PLAYING AT HERE? IF WE STEAL YORICK, THE AMERICANS WILL GO TO WAR TO GET HIM BACK.›

‹WE SHOULD BE SO LUCKY.›

MAN, THIS PLACE IS LIKE *SMALLVILLE* UPSTAIRS, *FORTRESS OF SOLITUDE* DOWNSTAIRS.

YOU CLEAN UP GOOD, YORICK.

COME, ENJOY HOT MUSH IN BAG WITH ME.

OH, GOD, NOT *M.R.E.s*. I LIVED OFF THOSE THINGS FOR A *WEEK* ON MY WAY TO D.C. THE SUPER-MARKETS HAD ALL BEEN RANSACKED, BUT I FOUND SOME DEAD GUY IN PENNSYLVANIA WITH AN OLD *Y2K BUNKER* IN HIS BACKYARD.

FAT LOT OF GOOD PREPARING FOR THE WORST DOES, HUH? EVERY BOY SCOUT THEY TAUGHT TO "BE PREPARED" IS A *CORPSE* NOW.

THANK-FULLY, THAT'S ALSO THE *GIRL* SCOUTS' MOTTO.

I WAS A BROWNIE.

HEATHER AND HEIDI JUST GAVE US A NICKEL TOUR OF THE LOWER LEVEL, AND THEY SEEM *PERFECT*.

THE SPACE CADETS CAN THEORETICALLY SURVIVE DOWN THERE FOR YEARS, UNTIL WE'RE SURE THE PLAGUE'S DISSIPATED.

OR UNTIL DR. MANN COMES UP WITH SOME KIND OF VACCINE.

NO! NOT ACCEPTABLE!

UNITED NATIONS CHARTER SAY, "IF, OWING TO ACCIDENT, DISTRESS, EMERGENCY OR UNINTENDED LANDING, THE PERSONNEL OF A SPACECRAFT LAND IN TERRITORY UNDER THE JURISDICTION OF A CONTRACTING PARTY, THEY SHALL BE SAFELY AND PROMPTLY RETURNED TO REPRESENTATIVES OF THE LAUNCHING AUTHORITY!"

WHAT THE...? *COOKIE MONSTER* SPEAKS BETTER ENGLISH THAN YOU. WHEN THE HELL DID YOU LEARN ALL THAT?

I HAVE LONG BOAT RIDE TO STATES FOR MEMORIZING.

WE HAVE NO INTENTION OF TAKING YOUR MAN *HOSTAGE*, NATALYA. WE'RE JUST HOLDING HIM FOR OBSERVATION.

FOR NOW, I DON'T WANT THE BOYS VENTURING BEYOND THIS SECTOR. YORICK AND AMPERSAND MAY BE IMMUNE TO WHATEVER CAUSED THIS, BUT THERE'S A CHANCE THEY'RE STILL--

BOOOM

WAS THAT...?

SOYUZ.

YOU SAID IT'S NOT SUPPOSED TO BE ENTERING THE ATMOSPHERE FOR ANOTHER *THREE HOURS*!

THEY MUST BE MOVE UP WINDOW TO AVOID STORM OR--

WHATEVER. GRAB YOUR GEAR, NATALYA.

LADIES, YOU'RE AT STANDBY ON THE AIRLOCKS DOWNSTAIRS.

DOCTOR, KEEP AN EYE ON YORICK.

I'D *NEVER* DO ANYTHING TO FUCK THIS UP, 355.

SCOUT'S HONOR.

⟨SHOULD WE BE WORRIED ABOUT THAT SMOKE?⟩

⟨NOT NECESSARILY. THE *R.S.C.* EGGHEADS TOLD ME THE SOFT-LANDING ENGINES MIGHT SINGE PART OF THE FIELD. THE CAPSULE CAN TAKE THE HEAT.⟩

⟨I'M A LITTLE CONCERNED ABOUT THE PLACEMENT, THOUGH. PILOTING THOSE TIN CANS ISN'T AN EXACT SCIENCE, BUT THEY'RE ABOUT THREE VERSTS OUTSIDE THE TARGET ZONE.⟩

⟨VERSTS?⟩

SORRY, IN THE ENGLISH, VERST IS ALMOST ABOUT, EHH... ONE KLICK.

⟨A *KLICK?* THAT'S A REAL WORD? I THOUGHT THEY ONLY USED THAT IN BAD VIETNAM MOVIES.⟩

⟨ARE YOU HIGH? OF COURSE IT'S REAL. A KLICK IS ONE KILOMETER... THAT'S .62 MILES IN *AMERICAN.*⟩

⟨I CAN HANDLE METRIC, SMARTASS. BUT I'VE BEEN PART OF A PARAMILITARY ORGANIZATION SINCE I WAS SIX-TEEN, AND I'VE *NEVER* HEARD ANYONE USE--⟩

MOTHERFUCK.

WHO THE FUCK ARE **YOU**?

MOVE AND YOU'RE **DEAD**!

WAIT!

I...I SURRENDER.

JUST DON'T HURT ANYONE ELSE. PLEASE.

YORICK...

TAKE HIM, LADIES. GET THE **MONKEY**, TOO.

YOU SURE ABOUT THAT?

SHE HAS **AIDS**. AND SHE **BITES**.

AR OH

⟨MA'AM?⟩

⟨FINE, LEAVE THE DAMN ANIMAL WITH THE WOMAN.⟩

⟨JUST **MOVE**!⟩

STUPID.

TRISTA... *PYATDESYAT*...

THREE HUNDRED, IS...IS YOU DEAD?

NATALYA. ARE YOU...?

〈I'LL ⸗EHN⸗ LIVE. I'M SO SORRY. CAN'T BELIEVE I FUCKING PASSED OUT. LIKE IT'S MY *FIRST* TIME GETTING SHOT. ARE THE OTHERS--〉

〈I DON'T KNOW, BUT I THINK THEY GOT YORICK.〉

〈A RADIO. ONE OF THEM HAD A *RADIO*...〉

〈THERE.〉

WHOEVER THIS IS, TURN YOUR CRAFT AROUND AND BRING THE MALE BACK *NOW*.

⸗KZACK⸗

AGENT 355, IS IT...?

73

JESUS, MY GAUGES ARE BURIED SO DEEP IN THE RED, SOME OF THEM HAVE GONE *GREEN* AGAIN.

YOU THINK THE WOMEN WILL THROW A PARADE FOR US, VLAD?

I SHOULD HOPE SO, SIR. ONE TO RIVAL GAGARIN'S IN '61.

I KNOW WHY YOU BOYS ARE JOKING, BUT I'M TELLING YOU THAT YOU *SHOULD* BE STRESSED. IF WE CAN'T KEEP SHOCK NEUTRALIZATION ONLINE--

WHO DO YOU THINK THEY'LL HAVE WAITING FOR US DOWN THERE, VLAD? SOME OF THOSE SEXY NURSES?

PERHAPS A FEW OF YOUR CHEERLEADERS.

One Small Step
Chapter Four

I DON'T THINK SO.

BRIAN K. VAUGHAN PIA GUERRA
Writer/Co-Creators/Penciller

JOSE MARZAN, JR., Inker

Clem Robins, Letterer   Pamela Rambo, Colorist

Zylonol, Separator J.G. Jones, Cover Artist

Zachary Rau, Ass't Editor   Will Dennis, Editor

Y: THE LAST MAN CREATED BY
BRIAN K. VAUGHAN AND PIA GUERRA

Oldenbrook, Kansas
Now

SHUT THE HELL UP, NATALYA!

<WHAT RIGHT DO YOU HAVE TO SURRENDER MY MAN? I TRAVELED ACROSS A GODDAMN OCEAN TO RETURN OUR ONE FUCKING COSMONAUT TO-->

IF YOU DON'T SHUT YOUR MOUTH, YOU'RE GOING TO HAVE A SECOND BULLET IN YOU. AND I GUARANTEE I'M A BETTER SHOT THAN THEY WERE.

IS EVERY-THING ALL RIGHT, AGENT?

LISTEN CAREFULLY, MY TEAM AND I ARE GOING TO PICK UP THE MEN AT THEIR EMERGENCY LANDING ZONE AND BRING THEM BACK TO THE FACILITY WHERE YOU STOLE YORICK.

YOU'LL MEET US THERE LATER TONIGHT, AND WE'LL MAKE THE TRADE.

YOU ASSUME THAT I THINK YOUR STORY IS TRUE.

BESIDES, EVEN IF IT WERE, WHY WOULD YOU SACRIFICE TWO GROWN MEN FOR ONE SCRAWNY BOY?

HEY! ASSHOLE! THIS BAG ISN'T SOUNDPROOF!

BECAUSE, I'M... I'M IN LOVE WITH HIM.

SHE'S WHAT?

WELL... THIS IS FINALLY STARTING TO MAKE SENSE.

FINE THEN, WE WILL MEET YOU TONIGHT. BUT IF YOUR SPACESHIP FAILS TO APPEAR...YOU WILL NEVER SEE YOUR BOYFRIEND AGAIN.

ALTER OUT.

‹PILOT, SET US DOWN!›

‹WE HAVE WORK TO DO...›

⟨YOU DESPERATE FUCKING IDIOT. THEY'LL **NEVER** GIVE YOU YORICK BACK!⟩

⟨THEY'RE GOING TO TAKE MY COUNTRY'S ONLY MAN FOR THEMSELVES AND **SLAUGHTER** THE REST OF US! AND FOR WHAT, SOME STUPID **CRUSH?**⟩

DON'T BE DENSE, NATALYA. I'M NOT LETTING THEM TAKE YOUR COSMONAUT, AND I'M **DEFINITELY** NOT IN LOVE WITH YORICK.

I ONLY SAID THAT TO GET THEM BACK HERE.

⟨SORRY, MY ENGLISH MUST **BLOW**...I THOUGHT YOU JUST SAID THAT YOU'RE DELIBERATELY LURING AN ENTIRE **PLATOON** BACK TO THE PEOPLE WHO **KILLED** TWO OF THEIR SOLDIERS!⟩

355!

DR. MANN!

THEY... THEY GOT YORICK.

I KNOW. IS EVERYONE OKAY?

I'LL LIVE, BUT THOSE THUGS TOSSED HEATHER AND HEIDI A PRETTY GOOD BEATING ON THEIR WAY INSIDE THE COMPOUND.

DID...DID WE JUST GET RAIDED BY **ISRAELIS?**

WHY? I MEAN, WE'RE **JEWISH!**

WE'LL WORRY ABOUT MOTIVES LATER. RIGHT NOW, I NEED YOU TO FIX NATALYA'S SHOULDER AS BEST YOU CAN.

WE HAVE WORK TO DO...

IT'S A TRAP!

SHE...SHE MADE UP THAT BULLSHIT ABOUT *NASA* DUDES TO *TRICK* YOU. LET'S JUST GET OUT OF HERE AND PROCEED WITH THE TORTURING OR WHATEVER.

〈THE MORE HE OBJECTS, THE MORE I *BELIEVE* THE AMERICAN GIRL'S ASSERTION.〉

〈I'M NOT SURE, ALTER. IT STILL SOUNDS PREPOSTEROUS TO ME.〉

〈EITHER WAY, A BOY IN THE HAND IS WORTH TWO IN THE BUSH, NO?〉

〈SADIE, IF ANY-ONE OTHER THAN ISRAEL ACQUIRES MALES, OUR NATION LOSES THE LEVERAGE AND POSITION THAT COME WITH HAVING YORICK.〉

〈SO WHAT, YOU'RE GOING TO HOLD ON TO THE BOY *AND* MAKE A PLAY FOR THE ASTRONAUTS?〉

〈I'M DOING WHAT I HAVE TO DO.〉

〈BUT YORICK'S PROBABLY *RIGHT* ABOUT THE AMERICANS SETTING A TRAP INSIDE THAT BARN!〉

〈THAT'S WHY WE'RE TAKING THE FIGHT *OUTSIDE.*〉

〈NAIM, I WANT YOU TO LEAD THE REST OF THE UNIT BACK TOWARDS THE FACILITY WE STORMED. FROM A SAFE DISTANCE, SHADOW THE AMERICANS TO THE LANDING ZONE.〉

〈THE CULPER RING AGENT HAS ONE OF OUR HANDHELDS, SO MAINTAIN RADIO SILENCE UNTIL I CONTACT YOU WITH FURTHER INSTRUCTIONS.〉

〈BEHATZLACHA!〉

⟨I SHOULD GO WITH THEM, ALTER. THOSE GIRLS ARE BARELY FIELD RATED, AND NAIM ISN'T EXACTLY *LEADERSHIP MATERIAL*.⟩

⟨I WANT YOU WITH ME, SADIE.⟩

⟨IF THIS 355 IS SMART, SHE'S ALREADY DISPATCHED PART OF HER TEAM TO LOOK FOR YORICK. IT WILL TAKE US BOTH TO GUARD HIM.⟩

UM, I MAY NOT SPEAK HEBREW, BUT IT'S PRETTY CLEAR WHEN YOU'RE TALKING ABOUT *ME*. ALL I HEAR IS, "GIBBERISH GIBBERISH *YORICK* GIBBERISH."

YOU'RE A HEARTBEAT AWAY FROM BEING GAGGED, MR. BROWN.

AND I THINK THAT I'M STARTING TO UNDERSTAND THIS BLACK SACK ROUTINE, TOO.

IT'S NOT ABOUT KEEPING ME IN THE DARK, RIGHT? IT'S ABOUT HELPING YOU PRETEND THAT I'M JUST AN *OBJECT* AND NOT A--

IF I REMOVE IT, WILL YOU PROMISE TO STOP BLABBERING?

OW. PUPILS... *CONSTRICTING*.

⟨SADIE, KEEP A CLOSE EYE ON OUR GUEST.⟩

APPARENTLY, HE FANCIES HIMSELF QUITE THE ESCAPE ARTIST.

OOO, AM I SUPPOSED TO BE IMPRESSED BY YOUR SCARY "INTEL"?

EVERYONE WHO'S READ MY AWARD-WINNING *NEWSLETTER* KNOWS WHAT I DO.

NO, YOU'RE SUPPOSED TO BE IMPRESSED BY THE *HANDCUFFS* YOU'VE BEEN TRYING TO FREE YOURSELF FROM FOR THE LAST HOUR.

THEY WERE DESIGNED BY MOSSAD TO BE ONE HUNDRED PERCENT UNPICKABLE.

THE ONLY PALESTINIAN EVER TO BREAK OUT OF MEGIDDO PRISON STILL HAD TO SAW OFF HIS LEFT HAND TO GET OUT OF--

ARE YOU TAUNTING ME WITH A MANIACAL *DEATHTRAP?* WHAT ARE YOU, A *BATMAN VILLAIN?*

SERIOUSLY, I THOUGHT YOU PEOPLE WERE SUPPOSED TO BE THE *GOOD GUYS.*

NO MATTER WHAT STUPID SHIT YOUR PRIME MINISTER EVER DID, MY PARENTS WERE ALWAYS HUGE SUPPORTERS OF ISRAEL. I MEAN, DO YOU EVEN KNOW WHO MY *MOTHER* IS?

〈BETTER THAN YOU DO, I SUSPECT.〉

WHAT DID YOU JUST SAY? DID YOU JUST INSULT MY *MOM?* SAY IT IN ENGLISH, G.I. JANE, I *DARE* YOU!

〈CUFF HIM TO ONE OF THE CHAIRS INSIDE THE COPTER.〉

〈IF HE REFUSES TO BE SILENT, KNOCK HIM *UNCONSCIOUS.*〉

YOU SURE WE'RE IN THE RIGHT PLACE?

POSITIVE. ALL WE HAVE TO DO NOW IS WAIT.

I STILL DON'T UNDER-STAND WHY *I* HAD TO COME ALONG, 355.

I TOLD YOU, WE NEED THE TWINS ON CALL BACK AT THE HOT SUITE.

--IS DOING WHAT I *ASKED* HER TO DO, DOCTOR. IF MY PLAN WORKS, WE'LL BE ABLE TO HOLD ON TO THE ASTRONAUTS *AND* GET YORICK BACK.

BUT NATALYA--

AND IF IT DOESN'T?

⟨IS THAT HER, NAIM? IS SHE THE ONE WHO KILLED SELTZER AND KLARSFELD?⟩

⟨HOW THE HELL AM I SUPPOSED TO KNOW? BESIDES, WE'RE NOT HERE TO GET REVENGE.⟩

⟨NOT *YET*, ANYWAY...⟩

HEY, YOU SPEAK ENGLISH?

BE QUIET.

I'LL TAKE THAT AS A *YES*. LISTEN, YOU'RE OBVIOUSLY NOT CRAZY ABOUT THIS WHOLE CAMPAIGN. IT'S WRITTEN ALL OVER YOUR FACE.

MAYBE YOU THINK YOU'RE JUST FOLLOWING ORDERS HERE...BUT DON'T FORGET HOW THAT EXCUSE WENT OVER AT *NUREMBERG*.

IF YOU ARE TRYING TO WIN MY FAVOR, I WOULD ADVISE YOU AGAINST COMPARING ME TO PEOPLE WHO KILLED MY *GREAT GRAND-FATHER*.

OH.

BESIDES, THAT WOMAN TOOK A *BULLET* FOR ME IN HEBRON. HOW...HOW COULD I JUST BETRAY HER *NOW?* HOW COULD I--

SADIE!

GET OUT HERE. SOMETHING'S HAPPENING.

⟨WE DON'T HAVE TIME TO BE PRECIOUS ABOUT THIS, SADIE. WE ONLY NEED ONE MAN TO ENSURE OUR NATION'S SECURITY. OTHERS WOULD JUST BECOME LIABILITIES.⟩

⟨I ASKED YOU TO STAY WITH ME BECAUSE I KNOW YOU'RE--⟩

⟨PUT IT DOWN.⟩

⟨...INTERESTING.⟩

⟨I PRESUME YOU STILL REMEMBER THE PUNISHMENT FOR TREASON?⟩

⟨THIS HAS TO STOP, ALTER. I'M BEGINNING TO REALIZE THAT A NEVER-ENDING BATTLE IS JUST A...A WAR WITHOUT WINNERS.⟩

⟨YOU'RE MAKING A VERY BAD DECISION.⟩

⟨MAYBE, BUT AT LEAST I'M FINALLY MAKING ONE. THAT'S SOMETHING I SHOULD HAVE DONE A LONG TIME--⟩

HOLY SHIT!

WHAT WAS THAT?

KOFF KOFF KOFF

YOU FUCKING ANIMAL!

IF THAT MISSILE HAD HIT THOSE PEOPLE, I'D HAVE CHOKED THE LIFE RIGHT OUT OF YOUR GODDAMN--

〈NAIM... DON'T LET THEM...GET TO THE SPACE-CRAFT...〉

WHAT ARE YOU DOING?

STOP IT!

〈...TERMINATE...THE AMERICANS...〉

POOR DUMB KIDS.

LIKE HITTING FISHES IN BUCKET...

LISTEN UP! I'M SURE AT LEAST ONE OF YOU SPEAKS ENGLISH, SO SPREAD THE WORD!

AT THE COUNT OF THREE, I AM GOING TO STAND BACK UP. IF YOU HAVE ALL DROPPED YOUR WEAPONS AND PUT YOUR HANDS IN THE AIR, NO ONE ELSE WILL BE HARMED.

THIS IS NEVER GOING TO WORK, 355! THERE ARE LIKE A DOZEN OF THEM AND ONLY TWO OF--

IF YOU TRY TO KILL ME, YOU MIGHT SUCCEED, BUT MY SNIPER WILL STOP AIMING FOR APPENDAGES AND START HITTING *FACES*. THE CHOICE IS YOURS!

ONE... *TWO*...

THREE.

WOW.

COLLECT THEIR WEAPONS AND PUT THEM INTO ZIP TIES, DOCTOR. NATALYA HAS YOUR BACK, SO DON'T BE SCARED.

ISRAELI COMMAND, THIS IS AGENT 355. YOUR GREED JUST *INVALIDATED* OUR DEAL.

I'M CURRENTLY HOLDING YOUR ENTIRE REGIMENT HOSTAGE, AND WON'T RETURN THEM UNTIL I HAVE OUR MAN BACK.

THAT WAS YOUR MASTER PLAN, JOAN OF ARC? YOU REALLY THINK THIS LUNATIC WOULD HAVE TRADED *MOI* FOR A FEW WORTHLESS *GIRL GRUNTS?*

YORICK?

YOU *ESCAPED?*

WELL, THAT'S A RELATIVE TERM.

BUT FORGET ABOUT ME, WHAT'S THE WORD ON MAJOR TOM AND FRIENDS?

I'M NOT SURE YET. I KNEW THE ISRAELIS WOULD TRAIL US, SO WE LED THEM TO A *FAKE* LANDING ZONE. I'M HEADED FOR THE REAL ONE NOW.

I SEE SMOKE, BUT NATALYA SAID TO EXPECT THAT.

THING DID LOOK LIKE IT WAS COMING IN PRETTY FAST THOUGH, DIDN'T IT?

OKAY, I'M COMING UP ON IT AND--

HZZZ KZACK! EEEEEE

THAT'S NOT FUNNY, 355!

COME ON, KNOCK OFF THE "TO BE CONTINUED" SHIT! WHAT'S GOING ON?

HELLO?

Oldenbrook, Kansas
Now

355!

DR. MANN?! YOU'RE SUPPOSED TO BE GUARDING THE--

NATALYA'S GOT THE ISRAELIS UNDER CONTROL. SHE TOLD ME TO GIVE YOU A HAND WITH--

THEY'RE ALIVE!

WE *HAVE* TO HELP THEM!

NO!

BUT THEY'VE BEEN IN ZERO GRAVITY FOR *MONTHS!* THEY CAN'T WALK WITHOUT--

I'LL TAKE CARE OF IT, DOCTOR!

YOU JUST STAY THE HELL BACK!

ARE YOU ALL RIGHT?

HYDRAZINE LEAK... IN THE CABIN...

STAY CALM! {KOFF}

I'M GOING TO {KOFF} {KOFF} {KOFF}

COME ON! WE *NEED* TO GET THEM OUT OF HERE!

DOCTOR, I TOLD YOU--

UHF!

SHUT THE FUCK UP AND CARRY!

SLOW DOWN! WE CAN'T RISK TEARING THEIR SUITS! IF WHATEVER KILLED ALL THE MEN IS STILL IN THE ATMOSPHERE, IT COULD--

THEY SAID THERE'S A *HYDRAZINE LEAK*, GODDAMMIT! IF WE DON'T HURRY, THE WHOLE *SOYUZ* COULD--

IF THIS IS SOME KIND OF CHEAP *PLOY*...

NO. NO MORE GAMES. I'M TIRED OF PLAYING ARMY.

GO, HELP YOUR FRIENDS.

THEY *ARE* FRIENDS, RIGHT? NOT CAPTORS?

CAPTORS? OF COURSE NOT. WHO TOLD YOU...

IT DOESN'T MATTER. OUR INTELLIGENCE WAS POOR FOR THIS MISSION. NOT THAT IT EXCUSES OUR *ACTIONS*...

I PROMISE TO WAIT HERE WITH ALTER UNTIL YOUR PEOPLE DECIDE WHAT PUNISHMENT THE TWO OF US DESERVE.

I ONLY ASK THAT YOU SHOW MERCY TO THE OTHER GIRLS. THEY'RE NOT TO BLAME FOR OUR--

OH, SAVE THE *A FEW GOOD MEN* CRAP. ALL OF THE GOOD MEN ARE *DEAD*.

JUST TELL ME...WHY DID YOU PEOPLE DO THIS? AMERICA AND ISRAEL ARE SUPPOSED TO BE *FRIENDS*.

DON'T YOU KNOW? THIS IS WHAT HAPPENS TO FRIENDS WHEN A *MAN* COMES BETWEEN THEM.

ANYBODY HOME...?

AK AK AK

AHH!

OH...HEY, AMPERSAND.

NICE TO SEE YOU, TOO, BUDDY.

BUT WHAT IS THAT *SMELL* ON YOUR HANDS?

YORICK!

355.

YOU OKAY?

NOT EVEN CLOSE.

HOW'S OUR SPACE CADET?

RECOVERING DOWN IN THE HOT SUITE. DR. MANN AND THE TWINS THINK SHE'S GONNA BE FINE.

BUT YORICK, THE TWO MEN...

I KNOW, I HEARD. NATALYA FILLED ME IN ON THE WHOLE NIGHTMARE WHILE WE TOOK CARE OF THOSE ISRAELI SOLDIERS YOU CAPTURED.

WAIT, TOOK CARE OF THEM HOW?

WE MARCHED THEM BACK TO SADIE. SHE'S A TRAINED MEDIC, SO SHE CAN PATCH UP THE GIRLS YOU GUYS PUT HOLES IN.

WHO THE HELL IS *SADIE*?

THEIR NEW LEADER. THE OLD ONE'S BEEN HOGTIED AND COURT-MARTIALED OR WHATEVER, SO SADIE'S IN CHARGE NOW. SHE'S GOOD PEOPLE.

SHE HELPED *KIDNAP* YOU!

YEAH, AND THEN SHE HELPED ME ESCAPE.

SO WHAT, NOW WE'RE JUST SUPPOSED TO *LET THEM GO*?

WHAT CHOICE DO WE HAVE, 355? ARE WE GONNA BUILD A P.O.W. CAMP FOR THE WHOLE PLATOON?

BESIDES, NATALYA'S DESTROYING ALL OF THEIR WEAPONS AS WE SPEAK. THEY'RE BEATEN AND BROKEN, AND...AND ALL THEY CAN DO NOW IS HEAD BACK TO ISRAEL WITH THEIR TAILS BETWEEN THEIR LEGS, RIGHT?

THAT'S A PRETTY MAGNANIMOUS GESTURE COMING FROM THE GUY WHO WANTED TO LOCK UP EVERY WOMAN IN SIGHT BACK IN MARRISVILLE.

YEAH, I... I KNOW.

BUT IT WAS EITHER THAT OR LINE THEM UP IN FRONT OF A FIRING SQUAD.

AND I'VE HAD JUST ABOUT ALL THE DEATH I CAN TAKE FOR A WHILE.

BUT YORICK, THAT THING THAT ALMOST HIT THE SOYUZ...

DON'T WORRY, THAT WAS *ALTER,* NOT SADIE.

I TRIED TO STOP HER FROM FIRING IT, BUT I GUESS I ONLY MANAGED TO KNOCK THE MISSILE OFF COURSE.

HOLD ON, YOU TOOK DOWN A SOLDIER ARMED WITH A *ROCKET LAUNCHER?*

I KNOW, I'M SORRY. I SWEAR, I *TRY* TO STAY OUT OF TROUBLE, BUT--

YOU DON'T NEED TO *APOLOGIZE,* 'RICK. YOU SAVED A WOMAN'S *LIFE.*

WELL, THAT PRETTY MUCH DEFINES A *PYRRHIC* VICTORY, DOESN'T IT?

I MEAN, THE LAST TWO MEN WHO ACTUALLY HAD SOMETHING TO OFFER THE WORLD ARE *GONE.* NOW THE FATE OF HUMANITY IS BACK ON *MY* WORTHLESS SHOULDERS.

OH, KNOCK OFF THE SELF-DEPRECATING BULLSHIT.

I'M NOT SAYING I WANT YOU TO KEEP PULLING YOUR STUPID STUNTS, BUT YOU DID OKAY TODAY. YOU'RE A *HERO.*

CHRIST, PLEASE DON'T USE THAT WORD. IF THERE'S ONE THING I NEVER WANT TO BECOME...

OH, GOD.

YOUR *SISTER.* I DIDN'T MEAN...

FORGET IT.

I JUST HATE THE SOUND OF HER NAME.

RIGHT. I HAVE TO REMEMBER TO CALL THOSE SANDWICHES *SUBS*, NOT... YOU KNOW.

SMARTASS.

HEY, LET ME ASK YOU SOMETHING.

WHEN YOU WERE TRYING TO CONVINCE THE ISRAELIS TO GIVE ME BACK, AND YOU TOLD THEM THAT YOU WERE IN *LOVE* WITH ME, YOU... YOU DIDN'T *MEAN* IT, DID YOU?

NIGGA, *PLEASE*.

WHEW.

I WAS *HOPING* YOU'D SAY THAT.

HEH. YEAH...

DANGER!

BIOSAFETY LEVEL 4
AIR-LOCK DOOR/DECON SHOWER
NO ENTRY WITHOUT HAZMAT SUIT

DR. WEBER?

GOD, NO ONE'S CALLED ME THAT IN *MONTHS.*

CIBA IS FINE.

CIBA, I'M DR. MANN. I HELPED BRING YOU IN. MY CONDOLENCES ABOUT THE...THE...

EXCUSE ME?

THE L.O.C.V.

"LOSS OF CREW AND VEHICLE."

NASA NEVER MET A CATASTROPHE IT COULDN'T DISTILL INTO AN ACRONYM.

MY CREW-MATES. WERE YOU ABLE TO RECOVER ANY...ANY REMAINS?

NOT YET. THE TEMPERATURE OF THE BLAST...

IF IT'S ANY CONSOLATION, THEY DIED INSTANTLY.

NO OFFENSE, DOCTOR, BUT I DON'T THINK THAT PHRASE HAS EVER BEEN ANY CONSOLATION TO ANYONE.

CIBA, WHAT...WHAT HAPPENED?

EXPIRED CHEMICALS INSIDE THE SOYUZ CORRODED PART OF OUR BOAT'S INTERIOR. WE MADE IT THROUGH REENTRY OKAY, BUT ALL HELL BROKE LOOSE WHEN WE FIRED THE SOFT-LANDING ENGINES.

I REALIZE THAT, BUT...

FORGIVE ME IF THIS IS INDELICATE, BUT YOU THREE HAD RADIO CONTACT WITH THE RUSSIANS. YOU KNEW ABOUT THE PLAGUE, YOU KNEW ALL OF THE MEN WERE DEAD DOWN HERE...

...SO WHY DID THE TWO PRECIOUS MALES ON BOARD LET A USELESS WOMAN ESCAPE FIRST?

I'M SORRY.

NO, BELIEVE ME, I SCREAMED THE SAME THING, BUT THE BOYS WOULDN'T LISTEN.

AS SOON AS WE BLEW THE EXPLOSIVE BOLTS ON THE HATCH, JOE AND VLAD STARTED PUSHING ME OUTSIDE. THEY KEPT SAYING THE SAME THING OVER AND OVER...

"WOMEN AND CHILDREN FIRST."

A *BABY*?

DO WE KNOW THE SEX YET?

SHE'S ONLY THREE WEEKS ALONG, TOO EARLY TO TELL.

BUT IF HER CHILD *IS* MALE, IT SHOULD BE FINE.

YOU BROUGHT THE MOTHER INSIDE IN AN UNCOMPROMISED SUIT, SO THEY THEORETICALLY HAVEN'T BEEN EXPOSED TO ANY POSSIBLE REMNANTS OF THE PLAGUE.

AND WE HAVE MORE THAN ENOUGH SUPPLIES FOR CIBA TO SPEND THE DURATION OF HER PREGNANCY IN A CLEAN ENVIRONMENT.

CLEAN, MAYBE, BUT NOT *SECURE*...IF THE ISRAELIS WERE ABLE TO FIND THIS PLACE, SO CAN OTHERS.

YEAH, BUT WE CAN'T EXACTLY BRING A PREGNANT LADY IN A SPACESUIT WITH US TO CALIFORNIA, CAN WE? THAT WOULD MAKE FOR A GREAT SITCOM, BUT A LOUSY ROAD TRIP.

WE CAN'T JUST LEAVE THESE PEOPLE ALONE AND DEFENSELESS, YORICK.

NO, YOU CANNOT...

...THIS IS WHY YOU WILL PLEASE BE LEAVING THEM IN THE COMPANY OF *ME*.

BECAUSE OF ISRAEL WOMENS, I NOW HAVE MANY OF BANGING ARTILLERY TO USE ON ANYONE WHO MIGHT BROUGHT TROUBLE IN.

MAN, I WOULD *LOVE* TO DIAGRAM THAT SENTENCE.

⟨NATALYA, WE CAN'T ASK YOU TO STAY. YOU'VE DONE SO MUCH ALREADY. YOU DESERVE TO GO *HOME*.⟩

⟨I APPRECIATE THE OFFER, PAL, BUT I CAN'T GO BACK TO RUSSIA, NOT EMPTY-HANDED.⟩

⟨BESIDES, I DEDICATED MY *LIFE* TO RETRIEVING OUR LAST MAN. NOW THAT HE'S PASSED, I'M A SHIP WITHOUT A RUDDER. LOOKING AFTER THIS KID MIGHT STOP ME FROM, YOU KNOW, *CAPSIZING*.⟩

WHAT ABOUT ME? SOMEONE WILL HAVE TO RUN TESTS AND COLLECT GENETIC SAMPLES AND--

MY SISTER AND I ARE MORE THAN QUALIFIED TO HANDLE THAT, DR. MANN. YOU SHOULD PRESS ON TO YOUR BACKUP LAB, CONTINUE YOUR RESEARCH ON YORICK AND HIS PET.

WHAT'S THE HURRY? WE CAN STICK AROUND LONG ENOUGH TO PASS OUT CIGARS AND SHIT, CAN'T WE? THERE MIGHT BE A BOUNCING BABY *BOY* ON THE WAY!

IF THE FETUS **IS** MALE, WE CAN'T KEEP ALL OF OUR EGGS IN ONE BASKET...OR SPERM IN ONE BARN, AS THE CASE MAY BE.

WE HAVE TO GET YORICK OUT OF HERE **ASAP.**

SORRY, LADIES, I GUESS THAT'S OUR CUE. WE LIKE TO STORM INTO TOWN, INFLICT MAXIMUM DAMAGE, AND THEN DISAPPEAR...LIKE A **KISS** CONCERT.

ONLY WITH LESS UNINTENDED PREGNANCIES IN OUR WAKE.

HEY, IT WAS NICE OF YOU TO BRING A LITTLE EXCITEMENT OUR WAY, DOCTOR.

DOSVIDANYA, ZAMYATIN. I WISH I COULD HAVE HEARD THE STORY BEHIND THAT GOLD STAR OF YOURS.

〈AND PERHAPS YOU STILL WILL.〉

〈UNTIL THEN, KEEP YOUR POWDER DRY AND ALL THAT.〉

LATER, NATALYA. THANKS FOR, WELL, "HOPE" IS A CORNY WORD, BUT--

YOU ARE GOOD BOY, YORICK.

WHEN YOU ARE DONE, YOU MAY EVEN BE OKAY **MAN.**

⟨I'M SORRY ABOUT THIS, ALTER, BUT IT DOES MAKE THINGS EASIER.⟩

⟨TELL ME, SADIE, HOW DO YOU THINK THE LEGION OF WOMEN STILL LOYAL TO ME IN ISRAEL WILL HANDLE YOUR LITTLE *COUP?*⟩

⟨I SUPPOSE WE'LL CROSS THAT BRIDGE WHEN WE MAKE IT BACK HOME...*IF* WE MAKE IT. WE STILL HAVE TO REPAIR THE TROOP TRANSPORT AND--⟩

⟨COLONEL, SECURE FREQUENCY FOR YOU.⟩

⟨WHAT DID WE DISCUSS, NAIM? NO MORE RANKS.⟩

⟨SORRY, UM, *SADIE.*⟩

⟨IT'S THE AMERICAN POLITICIAN.⟩

⟨NO, WE'RE DONE BEING MANIPULATED BY WOMEN WHOSE POWER HAS MADE THEM *PARANOID.*⟩

⟨SO WHAT SHOULD I DO?⟩

⟨TELL HER WE HAVE ONLY ONE THING TO SAY TO HER...⟩

Washington, D.C.
Now

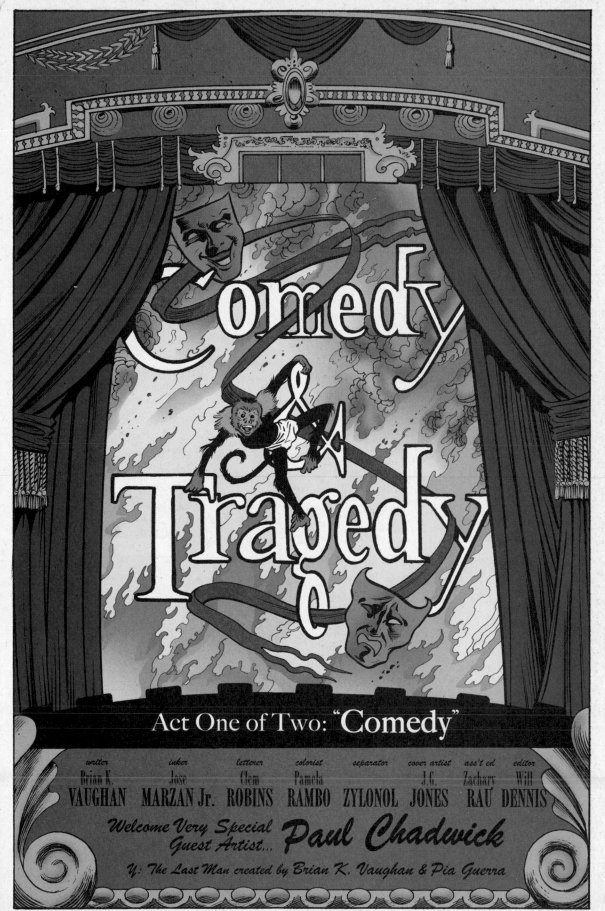

Act One of Two: "Comedy"

writer — Brian K. VAUGHAN
inker — Jose MARZAN Jr.
letterer — Clem ROBINS
colorist — Pamela RAMBO
separator — ZYLONOL
cover artist — J.G. JONES
ass't ed — Zachary RAU
editor — Will DENNIS

Welcome Very Special Guest Artist... Paul Chadwick

Y: The Last Man created by Brian K. Vaughan & Pia Guerra

ALL IS READY, FREDERIC, YOUR CREW AWAITS YOU!

WHAT THE...?

GOD-DAMMIT, MANDA!

YOU'RE NOT SUPPOSED TO ENTER UNTIL *AFTER* THE SONG!

HUH? OH, SORRY, EDIE. THIS...THIS IS MY FIRST PLAY, 'MEMBER?

WEREN'T BOTH OF YOUR FATHERS *GAY*?

YOU SHOULD HAVE A FUCKING *GENETIC PREDISPOSITION* FOR MUSICAL THEATER.

DON'T TALK ABOUT MY DADS!

HO HO, YOU REALLY WANNA TAKE ON EIGHT CREDITS OF STAGE COMBAT FROM STELLA ADLER?

TASTE IRON, SHORTIE!

KNOCK IT OFF, GIRLS!

SAVE THE CATTY SHIT FOR BROADWAY, EDIE.

THE REST OF YOU, LET'S TAKE FIVE!

SORRY, CAYCE, BUT IF WE'RE GONNA KEEP PICKING UP LITTLE ORPHAN ANNIES IN EVERY TOWN WE HIT, IT WOULD BE NICE IF ONE OF THEM COULD ACTUALLY *ACT* LIKE ANNIE.

GROW UP, EDIE.

YOU'RE JUST JEALOUS BECAUSE MANDA'S VOCAL RANGE SPANS MORE THAN *ONE OCTAVE.*

CAYCE, LUV, ARE YOU SURE ABOUT THIS FENCING BUSINESS? IT'S NOT IN THE SCRIPT, AND IT DOES STRIKE ME AS BEING RATHER... *GRATUITOUS.*

BESIDES, IT'S NOT AS IF THERE WILL EVER BE ANY *MALES* IN OUR AUDIENCE. WOMEN ARE MORE INTERESTED IN DRAMA AND ROMANCE THAN PUNCHING AND KICKING.

YOU CAN'T MAKE GENERALIZATIONS LIKE THAT, HENRIETTA! NOW THAT ALL OF THE MEN ARE GONE, WE HAVE TO START *EXPLODING* MYTHS ABOUT GENDER AND--

Um... EXCUSE ME?

ARE YOU PEOPLE THE PLAY ACTORS?

I...I WAS GIVEN A **FLYER.**

YES, MA'AM. WE'RE THE HUMBLE MEMBERS OF THE FISH & BICYCLE TRAVELING THEATER TROUPE. I'M OUR DIRECTOR AND SOMETIMES PLAYWRIGHT, CAYCE THOMAS.

YOU MUST BE THE MAYOR OF...FORGIVE ME, WHERE THE HELL ARE WE AGAIN?

NORTHLAKE. **NEBRASKA.** AND I WOULDN'T EXACTLY CALL MYSELF A MAYOR... MORE LIKE A **DEN MOTHER.** HEH.

SO, YOU FOLKS PUT ON SHOWS AND WHATNOT?

WE TRY OUR BEST. MY COMPANIONS AND I REPRESENT A CONFEDERATION OF CREATORS AND PERFORMERS WHO BANDED TOGETHER AFTER THE PLAGUE STRUCK.

WITH THE LACK OF DEPENDABLE ELECTRICITY THROUGHOUT THE COUNTRY, WE REALIZE THAT MOVIES, TELEVISION AND EVEN RADIO ARE LARGELY UNAVAILABLE, SO WE BRING OUR LO-TECH BRAND OF ART FROM TOWN TO TOWN AND--

DO YOU TAKE REQUESTS?

AH... _WHAT?_

YOU SEE, A LOT OF THE GIRLS AND I WERE FANS OF A PROGRAM CALLED AS THE WORLD TURNS.

I KNOW IT MIGHT SOUND SILLY, BUT WE WERE HOPING THAT YOU COULD PICK UP WHERE SOME OF THE STORYLINES LEFT OFF AND--

THAT'S...NOT REALLY WHAT WE DO, MA'AM.

ARE YOU SURE?

BECAUSE I BROUGHT SIX MONTHS' WORTH OF THE SOAP OPERA DIGEST.

IF YOU COULD JUST ACT OUT WHAT HAPPENED TO LLOYD THE BARTENDER AND THAT PRETTY KATE GIRL--

WOULDN'T YOU RATHER SEE SOMETHING A BIT MORE...ARTISTIC?

HOW ABOUT PIRATES OF PENZANCE?

IT'S A KICK-ASS GILBERT & SULLIVAN MUSICAL, A SATIRE ABOUT A SHELTERED YOUNG MAN WHO GETS SWEPT UP IN AN ADVENTURE WITH--

THE ONLY MUSICAL I'VE EVER SEEN IS THAT MOULIN ROUGE.

I...DIDN'T REALLY CARE FOR IT.

WELL, WE, UH, ALSO HAVE A VERY THOUGHT-PROVOKING ALL-FEMALE PRODUCTION OF MAMET'S GLENGARRY GLEN ROSS.

THAT WOULDN'T HAVE ANY SWEARS IN IT, WOULD IT?

ACTUALLY, HOW ABOUT IF WE GO AHEAD AND PICK A PLAY *FOR* YOU? I PROMISE WE'LL FIND A PERFECT FIT.

IF YOU SAY SO.

AS FOR THE COST...?

NOT TO WORRY, WE'RE A STRICTLY NON-PROFIT ORGANIZATION. ALL WE ASK IS A DONATION OF ONE CANNED FOOD ITEM PER AUDIENCE MEMBER.

AND PREFERABLY SOMETHING OTHER THAN *CUTTLEFISH*, PLEASE.

WE GOT STUCK WITH EIGHTY CANS OF THAT BARF DURING A RUN OF *ARCADIA* IN CHEYENNE.

OH, THAT SHOULDN'T BE A PROBLEM.

NORTHLAKE IS THE CANNING FACTORY CAPITAL OF NEBRASKA. WE HAVE ENOUGH FOOD TO LAST US UNTIL KINGDOM COME.

WHAT WE *DON'T* HAVE IS ENTERTAINMENT.

OUR LIBRARY'S BEEN PRETTY WELL PILLAGED, AND THE GIRLS COULD SURE USE A BIT OF AN ESCAPE.

OF COURSE, I... I UNDERSTAND.

THERE'S A SMALL PLAYHOUSE IN TOWN SQUARE. IT'S NOT MUCH, BUT WE SHOULD HAVE ENOUGH GAS TO POWER THE FOOTLIGHTS FOR A FEW NIGHTS. AS FOR ACCOMMODATIONS, I'M AFRAID WE'RE SHORT ON--

WE'RE MORE THAN HAPPY TO SLEEP UNDER THE STARS, MA'AM.

FOR NOW, LET'S SAY THAT WE'LL DEBUT THIS FRIDAY EVENING, AND PLAN FOR AN ENCORE ON SATURDAY, MAYBE A SUNDAY MATINEE IN CASE OF OVERFLOW.

MARVELOUS! GOD BLESS YOU GOOD PEOPLE FOR YOUR SERVICE! I'LL HAVE SOME OF MY HOMEMADE HOTCAKES WAITING AT THE PLAYHOUSE TOMORROW MORNING!

EXPLODING MYTHS ABOUT GENDER, EH?

YEAH... KA-BOOM.

TROUBLE SLEEPING, FEARLESS LEADER?

HEY, HENRIETTA. I WAS JUST TRYING TO FIND A WAY TO MAKE OUR PENZANCE PRODUCTION MORE, I DON'T KNOW...*RELEVANT.*

GOOD LORD, THAT HARDLY SOUNDS LIKE A BATTLE WORTH FIGHTING.

I WAS THINKING ABOUT REPLACING OUR PIRATES WITH THOSE "DAUGHTERS OF THE AMAZON" WE KEEP HEARING ABOUT.

THE ONES WHO SUPPOSEDLY TORCHED ALL THE SPERM BANKS?

I'M NOT SURE HOW KEEN DONNA REED AND FRIENDS WOULD BE TO SEE A BUNCH OF ONE-TITTED LESBIAN WARRIORS PRANCING AROUND STAGE. BESIDES, I THOUGHT THE AMAZONS WERE JUST ANOTHER URBAN LEGEND.

THAT'S ALL *ANYONE* WANTS THESE DAYS! DON'T THEY UNDERSTAND, THE ONLY WAY WE'RE EVER GOING TO *ESCAPE* THE ABSOLUTE FUCKING HORROR OF THE SITUATION WE'RE IN IS TO *CONFRONT* IT!

WE DON'T NEED ART THAT *PACIFIES*, WE NEED ART THAT *CHALLENGES* AND--

YEAH...YEAH, YOU'RE PROBABLY RIGHT.

DON'T BREAK YOUR BACK FOR THESE WOMEN, CAYCE. YOU HEARD THE LADY, THEY JUST WANT A LITTLE *ESCAPISM.*

AIEEEEEE

WAS THAT...?

MANDA.

MANDA!

MANDA, SWEETIE, WHERE ARE--

EDIE!

WHAT DID YOU DO TO HER?

I...I HEARD A NOISE OUT THERE.

SOUNDED LIKE A MONSTER.

DON'T BLAME ME, THE BRAT WOKE US ALL UP! SHE JUST STARTED SCREAMING!

OH, PRECIOUS, IT WAS PROBABLY JUST ONE OF OUR *HORSES.*

NUH-UH! I *KNOW* WHAT HORSES SOUND LIKE!

THIS WAS SOMETHING *BAD.* I THINK IT WAS THE... THE THING THAT KILLED ALL THE BOYS.

MANDA, A *MONSTER* DIDN'T MAKE THE MEN DIE.

THEN WHAT DID?

GOD?

AH...

WE STILL DON'T *KNOW,* MANDA. NO ONE DOES.

IT'S A...A MYSTERY.

THAT'S NOT TRUE.

I *KNOW* WHAT CAUSED THE PLAGUE.

EDIE, BE A DEAR AND *BUGGER OFF*, WILL YOU?

YOU'LL GIVE THE CHILD NIGHTMARES.

WE'LL ALL SLEEP BETTER ONCE WE ACCEPT THE *TRUTH*.

DO YOU KNOW WHO THE MOST FAMOUS ACTRESS OF SHAKESPEARE'S LIFETIME WAS?

WHAT THE HELL DOES THAT HAVE TO DO WITH ANYTHING?

IT'S A TRICK QUESTION. THERE *WERE* NO ACTRESSES DURING SHAKESPEARE'S LIFETIME.

EXACTLY. WOMEN WEREN'T ALLOWED ON STAGE, SO MALES HAD TO PLAY *BOTH* SEXES.

NO KIDDING, EDIE, WE ALL TOOK INTRO TO DRAMA HISTORY.

THEN YOU KNOW WHAT *ELSE* HAPPENED DURING SHAKESPEARE'S LIFETIME.

YOU KNOW WHAT CLOSED DOWN ALL THE THEATERS AND KILLED, LIKE, MILLIONS OF PEOPLE.

THE BLACK DEATH.

BINGO. AND WHEN DID THE BLACK DEATH FINALLY DISAPPEAR?

IN 1670 ... RIGHT AFTER WOMEN WERE ALLOWED BACK ON STAGE.

WHAT ARE YOU SUGGESTING, THAT THE BLACK DEATH WAS SOME KIND OF *PUNISHMENT*... FOR KEEPING WOMEN OUT OF *THEATER*?

THINK ABOUT IT, A LOT OF ANTHROPOLOGISTS OR WHATEVER BELIEVE THAT THE FIRST PERFORMERS WERE WOMEN, RIGHT? DRAMA IS IN OUR *BLOOD.*

SO STOPPING US FROM ACTING IS UNNATURAL, AND SCREWING WITH THE NATURAL ORDER ALWAYS MESSES SHIT UP.

BUT WHAT ABOUT *OUR* PLAGUE? THERE WAS NOTHING PREVENTING ANY OF *US* FROM ACTING WHEN IT HAPPENED.

BULL*SHIT!* HOW MANY *GOOD* ROLES WERE OUT THERE FOR WOMEN YOUR AGE BEFORE ALL THE MEN *DIED,* HENRIETTA?

WELL...

HOW MANY GOOD ROLES WERE OUT THERE FOR *ANY* OF US? UNLESS YOU WERE NINETEEN, WILLING TO SHOW YOUR BOOBS, AND/OR JULIA ROBERTS, WHAT DID WE HAVE?

I'M NOT SAYING I'M HAPPY THAT ANYBODY CROAKED, BUT IF YOU ASK ME, THIS WHOLE CATASTROPHE WAS JUST MOTHER NATURE'S WAY OF EVENING THE SCORE.

THAT IS THE MOST OUTRAGEOUS, EGOCENTRIC, *STUPID* THING I HAVE EVER--

HRRRREEE

I...I THINK IT'S *BACK.*

MUST HAVE ESCAPED FROM A ZOO.

NAH, MONKEYS DON'T WEAR *DIAPERS* AT THE ZOO.

THIS HAS GOT TO BE ONE OF THOSE HELPER MONKEYS. YOU KNOW, THE ONES DISABLED PEOPLE SOMETIMES HAVE? ITS MASTER PROBABLY DIED IN THE PLAGUE.

EREE

OH CHRIST, IT'S *BLEEDING.*

DON'T BE SCARED, CUTIE.

CAYCE AND I ARE FRIENDS. WE'RE GONNA MAKE YOU ALL BETTER.

WE *ARE?*

EDIE, WHAT IF THAT THING HAS RABIES OR--

THERE, THERE, BABY.

MAMA'S NOT GONNA LET *ANY-BODY* HURT YOU.

CRAP.

GODDAMN BIOLOGICAL CLOCKS...

OKAY, LADIES, YOU'VE ALL HAD A CHANCE TO GAWK AT OUR NEW MASCOT. CALL IS AT EIGHT A.M. SHARP TOMORROW, SO LET'S GET SOME SHUTEYE.

AND NO MORE BAD THOUGHTS TONIGHT, RIGHT, KIDDO?

I GUESS...

WHAT'S THE PROGNOSIS, DR. DOLITTLE?

MUCH BETTER NOW THAT THE BEAST AND I ARE BOTH PROPERLY *PISSED.*

SERIOUSLY, STITCHING MONKEY FLESH BACK TOGETHER IS A WALK IN THE PARK COMPARED TO SEWING NINETEEN BLOODY *PIRATE COSTUMES* OUT OF THIN AIR.

WHAT DO YOU THINK HAPPENED, HANK? WAS SHE ATTACKED BY A DOG OR SOMETHING?

I SINCERELY DOUBT IT. THE CUT WAS CLEAN, BUT DEEP...LIKE SOMEONE OUT THERE TOOK A SWING AT HER WITH A *BUTCHER'S KNIFE* OR SOMETHING.

GREAT, SO MUCH FOR "NO MORE BAD THOUGHTS."

OUR ONLY CONCERN RIGHT NOW SHOULD BE THIS ANIMAL'S *STENCH*. WE DON'T HAVE ANY *MONKEY NAPPIES* IN WARDROBE, DO WE?

HOLD ON, THAT'S NOT A *REAL* DIAPER. IT'S JUST AN OLD *HANDKERCHIEF*.

IF IT'S MONOGRAMMED, MAYBE WE CAN FIND OUT WHO SHE BELONGED TO...

EWW. UNLESS THE OWNER'S NAME WAS *BROWN*, I DON'T THINK WE'RE GOING TO FIND ANY CLUES IN HERE. POOR GIRL HASN'T BEEN CHANGED IN DAYS.

ACTUALLY, I'M NOT SO SURE THIS POOR GIRL...*IS* A GIRL.

WHAT THE HELL DOES *THAT* MEAN?

SEE FOR YOURSELF.

I'M HARDLY AN EXPERT, BUT I'M FAIRLY CERTAIN THAT THIS CREATURE HAS *MALE* PLUMBING.

HOLY CRAP, SHE'S *RIGHT*.

THAT'S *IMPOSSIBLE*. MONKEYS PROBABLY JUST HAVE WEIRD ANATOMIES. MAYBE THAT'S AN ENLARGED CLITORIS OR--

EE EEE

OH.

YEAH, NEVER SEEN A LITTLE MAN IN THE BOAT DO *THAT* BEFORE.

BUT I THOUGHT THE PLAGUE KILLED *EVERY* MAMMAL WITH A Y CHROMOSOME. I MEAN, I LOST BOTH MY MALE CATS. AND ALL OF MY BOYFRIEND'S *STALLIONS* DIED.

HALF OF THE MICE IN MY APARTMENT FINALLY PASSED ON, AND I'D BEEN TRYING TO KILL THEM FOR *YEARS.*

SO THE PLAGUE AFFECTED EVERYTHING BUT *MONKEYS?* HOW THE FUCK DOES THAT MAKE ANY SENSE? ISN'T THEIR *DNA,* LIKE, ALMOST IDENTICAL TO OURS?

LORD, WHAT IF IT *DID* AFFECT MONKEYS...JUST NOT *THIS* ONE?

WHAT IF THIS IS THE *LAST MALE ON EARTH?*

YOU'RE STARTING TO SOUND LIKE *EDIE,* HENRIETTA.

BUBBLES HERE IS PROBABLY JUST SOME KIND OF FREAK ANOMALY...LIKE THE HANDFUL OF PEOPLE WHO ARE SUPPOSEDLY IMMUNE TO *HIV* INFECTION, YOU KNOW?

THAT STILL MAKES THIS AN *ENORMOUS* DISCOVERY. WE HAVE TO TELL--

NO! THIS STAYS BETWEEN THE THREE OF US.

IF WORD SPREADS, WOMEN MIGHT START HOLDING OUT HOPE THAT A *HUMAN* MALE IS ALIVE SOME-WHERE, TOO.

WHAT'S SO BAD ABOUT GIVING PEOPLE A LITTLE HOPE?

IT'S IRRESPONSIBLE! THE PROMISE OF SOME IMAGINARY LAST MAN WHO MIGHT COME ALONG AND... AND *SAVE US* JUST GIVES WOMEN ANOTHER EXCUSE TO BE *COMPLACENT.*

WE'RE GOING TO BE *GONE* WITHIN A GENERATION IF WE DON'T GET OFF OUR ASSES AND FIND A WAY TO SAVE OUR-SELVES! THAT'S THE MESSAGE OUR TROUPE IS SUPPOSED TO BE SPREADING!

HOW...BY PUTTING ON *PIRATE MUSICALS?*

I'M SORRY, CAYCE, BUT--

NO.

YOU'RE... YOU'RE ABSOLUTELY RIGHT.

SO...WE **ARE** GOING TO TELL THE OTHERS?

NO. WE'RE GOING TO DO A **PLAY** ABOUT IT.

A PLAY ABOUT A **MONKEY**?

A PLAY ABOUT THE LAST MAN ON EARTH.

AN ORIGINAL WORK?

WHY NOT? I'M GOING TO WRITE SOMETHING SET RIGHT HERE, RIGHT NOW...A STORY ABOUT A GROUP OF WOMEN WHO DISCOVER THE ONLY LIVING MAN.

IS THAT REALLY SUCH A GOOD IDEA, LUV? WON'T IT SEEM LIKE WE'RE EXPLOITING TRAGEDY FOR, WELL... THE PURPOSES OF **ENTERTAIN- MENT**?

BUT THIS WILL BE **MORE** THAN ENTERTAINMENT! THIS WILL BE **ART**! WE'LL BE USING FICTION TO...TO HELP US GET TO THE **TRUTH**!

IT'S THE PERFECT STORY TO CONVEY ALL OF THE IDEAS I'VE BEEN TRYING TO GET ACROSS ABOUT LIFE IN THE POST-PLAGUE WORLD!

IT'S LIKE THE GODS SENT ME MY OWN SMELLY LITTLE **MUSE**.

AND YOU CALL **ME** EGOCENTRIC...

Afternoon.

A Kitchen: A table, a chair, a jar of pickled artichoke hearts.

A lone figure enters.

This is **TERESA**, one of billions of women made a widow by the Plague.

But unlike so many of her friends, Teresa hasn't turned to drugs or alcohol, she hasn't contemplated suicide. She is a pillar of strength, an independent woman.

Because Teresa and her husband built a shelter in their basement after 9/11, she has enough food to last her more than a year.

Teresa will not die. She is a **survivor**.

But as she sits down to enjoy her lunch, Teresa is confronted with a problem…

She is unable to open the jar.

She strains and struggles, but to no avail.

That's when it hits her... opening jars was the one thing she always asked her **husband** to do.

She and her friends used to joke that it was the **only** thing men were good for.

And then, the enormity of the situation sets in.

Teresa realizes that her husband is never coming back.

None of the men are coming back.

She reacts the same way the rest of us did when **we** finally allowed this moment to happen.

AHHHHHHH!

KERAASH

Just then a singsong voice calls out:

♪ IT'S SO NICE TO HAVE A MAN AROUND THE HOUSE... ♪

149

THE FRANKENSTEIN CHICK?

BACK IN THE 1800'S, SHE WROTE THIS BOOK CALLED *THE LAST MAN*, ABOUT A TWENTY-FIRST CENTURY PLAGUE THAT KILLS EVERYONE EXCEPT FOR A GUY NAMED LIONEL.

FUCK... WHAT CAUSED IT?

THE PLAGUE? SHE NEVER REALLY GETS AROUND TO EXPLAINING IT. BUT IT'S NOT THE POINT OF HER STORY.

IT'S A CONDEMNATION OF THE... THE UNCHECKED *MASCULINITY* THAT WAS ALWAYS THREATENING TO DESTROY THE PLANET.

IT'S ABOUT THE FAILURE OF ART AND IMAGINATION TO SAVE THE WORLD.

WELL, THAT'S ALL VERY NICE, BUT I STILL DON'T UNDERSTAND *MY* CHARACTER'S MOTIVATION.

I MEAN, IF TERESA CAN'T OPEN THE JAR, WHY DOESN'T SHE JUST USE A PAIR OF LATEX DISHWASHING GLOVES? YOU GET A REAL NICE GRIP THAT WAY, AND IT MAKES IT SUPER-EASY TO--

NO KIDDING! BUT THIS ISN'T THE GODDAMN MARTHA STEWART HOUR! WE'RE NOT HERE TO GIVE HELPFUL HOUSEHOLD TIPS! THIS IS *DRAMA!* TERESA'S DILEMMA IS AN *ALLEGORY!*

JESUS, WHY IS EVERYONE ACTING LIKE THIS IS THEIR *FIRST* FUCKING PLAY?

CAYCE, LUV, PERHAPS NOW WOULD BE A GOOD TIME FOR A SHORT BREAK? YOU COULD PROBABLY DO WITH SOME FRESH AIR.

...FINE. BUT SOMEBODY SWEEP UP THOSE ARTICHOKES. MAYBE *CURIOUS GEORGETTE* HERE CAN EAT THEM FOR LUNCH.

MM MNN

CAYCE, BE GENTLE WITH THE GIRLS. THEY'VE BEEN WORKING TO GET OFF-BOOK ALL MORNING.

I DIDN'T WRITE IT, HENRIETTA, IT WROTE ITSELF.

FOR GOD'S SAKE, YOU WROTE THIS PIECE IN LESS THAN A *NIGHT*.

EXACTLY. YOU'VE BEEN ACTING LIKE A WOMAN POSSESSED EVER SINCE WE FOUND THIS ANIMAL. HE'S TURNED YOU INTO--

SHHHH!

RIGHT NOW, YOU, EDIE AND I ARE THE ONLY THREE PEOPLE ALIVE WHO KNOW THAT OUR MONKEY IS ACTUALLY A *HE*.

IF ANYONE ELSE FINDS OUT THAT WE STUMBLED ONTO A LIVING *MALE*, MASS HYSTERIA WILL SWEEP THROUGH NEBRASKA LIKE A FUCKING--

WHAT IS GOING *ON* HERE?

YOU'RE DOING A PLAY ABOUT A *MAN* WHO SURVIVED THE PLAGUE?

THAT'S RIGHT, MA'AM. WE--

WHEN I AGREED TO LET YOU PEOPLE USE OUR THEATER, YOU TOLD ME THAT YOU WOULD FIND SOMETHING *APPROPRIATE* TO PERFORM.

WELL, WHAT IN HEAVEN'S NAME IS APPROPRIATE ABOUT *YOUR* IDEA? OUR *SUFFERING* SHOULDN'T BE FODDER FOR YOUR...YOUR CRUEL *FLIGHTS OF FANCY* !

PERHAPS YOU MIGHT WAIT TO *SEE* THE SHOW BEFORE YOU PASS JUDGMENT?

I DON'T NEED TO! THE WOMEN OF NORTHLAKE WANT OLD-FASHIONED ENTERTAINMENT, NOT THIS KIND OF CRASS EXPLOITATION !

REALLY? BECAUSE THE FIRST TWO EVENINGS OF THIS "CRASS EXPLOITATION" ARE ALREADY COMPLETELY SOLD OUT.

I ASSURE YOU, WE HAVE NO INTENTION OF DISRESPECTING THE FATHERS, HUSBANDS, SONS AND BROTHERS THAT YOU--THAT *WE*--ALL LOST.

THIS IS A PROVOCATIVE PLAY, BUT IT'S ALL DONE IN VERY GOOD TASTE.

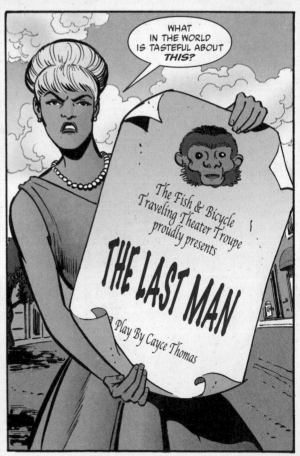

WHAT IN THE WORLD IS TASTEFUL ABOUT *THIS*?

The Fish & Bicycle Traveling Theater Troupe proudly presents

THE LAST MAN

A Play By Cayce Thomas

WHAT THE FU--

ER, THAT WAS EDIE'S DOING, CAYCE. SHE THOUGHT A PICTURE OF YOUR NEW PET WOULD MAKE FOR AN INTRIGUING *TEASER* POSTER.

THESE ARE PLASTERED ALL OVER TOWN!

THIS IS HOW YOU HONOR OUR DEAD... BY COMPARING MEN TO A SMILING *CHIMP*?

OF COURSE NOT. SEE, THIS MONKEY IS SORT OF THE...THE *SYMBOL* OF OUR THEATER COMPANY. IN CHINA, THEY REPRESENT, UH, CREATIVITY AND--

WE'RE NOT INTERESTED IN YOUR PRETENTIOUS GARBAGE.

WHY DON'T YOU PEDDLE YOUR *FILTH* ELSEWHERE?

BECAUSE WE HAVE A *RIGHT* TO EXPRESS OURSELVES.

AS DO I.

AND I HAVE EVERY INTENTION OF DOING JUST THAT.

WHAT DOES *THAT* MEAN?

IGNORE HER, CAYCE.

WHEN I DID THAT PLAY ABOUT A GAY JESUS, EVERY BLOODY SOCCER MOM WITH A PLACARD CAME OUT TO--

ARK ARK ARK

154

Opening Night
Eleven Hours Later

WELL, THIS IS GOING BETTER THAN EXPECTED.

AND NARY A SINGLE PROTESTOR OUTSIDE.

WE'RE NOT OUT OF THE WOODS YET. I MEAN, WE'RE STILL GIVING THE AUDIENCE WHAT THEY WANT. WAIT FOR US TO START *SUBVERTING* THEIR FANTASIES AFTER INTERMISSION...

GOOD SHOW OUT THERE, EDIE. YOU SOUND MORE LIKE A MAN THAN LEO DICAPRIO EVER DID.

WHATEVER, I'M DONE KISSING CHICKS IN PLAYS, THAT'S FOR SURE. MY CO-STARS KEEP "ACCIDENTALLY" SLIPPING ME THE TONGUE.

CAN YOU BLAME THEM? YOU'RE ALMOST CONVINCING ENOUGH TO MAKE *ME* WET... AND I'M THE ONE WHO SPIRIT-GUMMED THAT THING TO YOUR FACE.

NNN

SERIOUSLY, THIS IS ACTUALLY THE BEST I'VE FELT ABOUT A ROLE IN FOREVER, CAYCE. WE SHOULD THINK ABOUT TAKING THIS ONE ON THE ROAD.

YES, BREAK A LEG OUT THERE, LUV.

LET'S SEE IF WE CAN SURVIVE ACT TWO FIRST, ALL RIGHT?

IF ANYONE ELSE TRIES TO FRENCH ME, I'LL BREAK A LOT MORE THAN *THAT*!

‹DR. M, THIS IS TOYOTA.›

‹I'M AFRAID WE HAVE A PROBLEM.›

‹YOU'VE LOST THE ANIMAL AGAIN?›

‹NO, I'M RIGHT THE FUCK ON TOP OF IT. UNFORTUNATELY, SO ARE A BUNCH OF CIVVIES...PRETTY MUCH PERPETUALLY.›

‹I CAN RETRIEVE THE PACKAGE, BUT I CAN'T GUARANTEE THAT I WON'T OFF A FEW FRIENDLIES IN THE PROCESS.›

‹DAMMIT. THE LAST THING I NEED IS MORE BLOOD ON MY HANDS...›

‹STILL, I CAN'T GUARANTEE THAT WHATEVER GENETIC MATERIAL YOU WERE ALREADY ABLE TO CARVE OUT OF THE BEAST WILL BE ENOUGH.›

‹STAY IN POSITION FOR ANOTHER HOUR, TOYOTA. BUT ONLY MAKE A MOVE IF YOU CAN LIMIT THE NUMBER OF CASUALTIES TO NO MORE THAN ONE. I CAN'T JUSTIFY ANOTHER BODY COUNT.›

HAI, DOMO ARIGATO...

‹...YOU TIME-WASTING ASSHOLE.›

‹IF THERE'S ONE THING I HATE SITTING THROUGH, IT'S FUCKING *THEATER*...›

I'VE SEEN *ENOUGH!*

THIS PLAY IS A *MOCKERY!*

SIT DOWN!

NO, SHE'S RIGHT!

IT'S *OBSCENE!*

BE QUIET!

ARE WE REALLY GOING TO LET THESE PEOPLE PORTRAY WOMEN AS PETTY, VICIOUS *TRAMPS?*

YOU JUST INTERRUPTED MY FIGHT SCENE...

...YOU *FUCKING BITCH!*

162

LISTEN UP!

WE'RE LOOKING FOR THE CAPUCHIN MONKEY PICTURED HERE!

The Fish & Bicycle Traveling Theater Troupe proudly presents

THE LAST MAN

A Play By Cayce Thomas

WHY?

WHO ARE YOU PEOPLE?

WE'RE WITH W.H.O.

THAT'S RIGHT, THE WORLD HEALTH ORGANIZATION.

WHO?

AW, YOU GOT TO IT TOO FAST, 355. YOU WERE FOUR LINES AWAY FROM AN ABBOTT AND COSTELLO ROUTINE.

THAT ANIMAL IS A PUBLIC HEALTH RISK.

I'LL HAVE TO ASK YOU TO GIVE IT BACK TO US.

ABSOLUTELY NOT!

WE PATCHED UP WHATEVER YOU MONSTERS DID TO HIM. HE BELONGS TO US NOW.

HE?

OH. IT'S NOT REALLY A BOY.

IT'S A, UH, FEMALE WITH MALE GENITALIA... LIKE THAT ACTRESS, *WHAT'S-HER-NAME*.

I BEG YOUR PARDON!

WHICH ACTRESS WOULD *THAT* BE?

OH, NOT ONE OF *YOU*, THE ONE FROM ALL THOSE HORROR--

WHAT MY ASSOCIATE *MEANT* TO SAY IS THAT WE'VE BEEN WORKING ON GENETICALLY ENGINEERING A NEW BREED OF, UH...PLAGUE-RESISTANT *HERMAPHRODITES*.

UNFORTUNATELY, THE SPECIMENS WE'VE CREATED SO FAR--LIKE THE MONKEY THAT ESCAPED OUR FACILITY-- MIGHT ALSO BE CARRIERS OF A...A HIGHLY CONTAGIOUS *ASIAN FLU*.

OH.

IN THAT CASE...

WELCOME BACK, SHIT-SLINGER.

THAT'S THE LAST TIME WE TRUST *YORICK* TO KEEP AN EYE ON YOU.

HEY, I *TOLD* YOU, DR. MANN, WHEN I WOKE UP, AMPERSAND'S TRAVELING CASE WAS EMPTY, AND SOME *NINJA CHICK* WAS JUMPING OUT OF OUR TRAIN CAR.

NINJA CHICK.. RIIIIGHT...

THANK YOU FOR YOUR COOPERATION.

I APOLOGIZE FOR INTERRUPTING YOUR... PERFORMANCE.

HEY, IS THIS PLAY REALLY ABOUT THE LAST GUY ON EARTH?

DON'T WORRY, MA'AM, WE'VE ALREADY SHUT IT DOWN.

WHY DON'T I SHUT DOWN YOUR FAT *FACE*, DOUCHE NOZZLE?

YES, THIS WORK DOES INDEED DEAL WITH A GENTLEMAN SURVIVOR, AND THE PRODUCTION IS GOING TO HAVE A LONG, SUCCESSFUL RUN IN EVERY *OPEN-MINDED* CITY IN THE COUNTRY.

CAYCE HERE IS THE AUTHOR.

I WAS JUST WONDERING...HOW DOES IT END?